Prep, Cook, Freeze

A PALEO MEAL PLANNING COOKBOOK

Caroline Fausel

Creator of Olive You Whole

Written with Emily Steels

PAGE STREET
PUBLISHING CO.

PAGE STREET
PUBLISHING CO.

First published in 2021 by
Page Street Publishing Co.
27 Congress Street, Suite 105
Salem, MA 01970
www.pagestreetpublishing.com

Distributed by Macmillan, sales in Canada by The Canadian Manda Group.

26   25   24   23   22   1   2   3   4   5

ISBN-13: 978-1-64567-356-9
ISBN-10: 1-64567-356-1

Library of Congress Control Number: 2021931341

Cover and book design by Meg Baskis for Page Street Publishing Co.
Food photography by Becky Winkler
Author lifestyle photography by Amanda Proudfit
Written with Emily Steels

Printed and bound in the United States

DEDICATION

This cookbook is dedicated to my precious family. To my husband,
who has *always* supported my dreams and goals. And to my kiddos, you are
the entire reason this cookbook exists. I love you to the moon and back.

CONTENTS

FOREWORD

For some, cooking is a challenge. For others, like myself, the mere thought of deciding what to make for dinner can boggle the mind. Thankfully, Caroline's got us covered with her fabulous debut book.

I'm not surprised by this treasure trove of recipes, given the plethora of amazing dishes I've seen on Caroline's website, oliveyouwhole.com. She is a master at making classic, healthy Paleo dinners that are delightfully easy, and incredibly tasty too. Here, she takes things a step further, doing the meal planning for you, right down to grocery lists, prep steps and planning ahead.

Caroline's unique approach will save you so much time in the kitchen. You'll batch cook, then stash foods in the freezer, and thaw them out a couple of nights or weeks later so that dinner is ready in a few minutes. What could be better than that? Well, Sweet and Sour Hawaiian Meatballs (page 20), Teriyaki Sloppy Joes with Asian Slaw (page 19) and Best-Ever Barbecue Chicken Pizza (page 42), to name just a few of her down-to-earth yet elegant and easy dishes. She has reinvented scrumptious traditional fare for you in a healthy, simple fashion.

I can't think of anything better than these mouthwatering, healthy meals, especially given my own dietary restrictions. When I was diagnosed with celiac disease in 1998, I went on a gluten-free, Paleo diet. I wish this book had been around for me back then and am so thankful it is here now!

Caroline is a former vegetarian who came to healthy eating by figuring out what did not work for her. I have followed a similar path. By choosing to eat clean, wholesome Paleo food, I've healed myself and nourished my family. This is something else she and I have in common. While my children are decades older than hers, clean food and family meals are values we both hold dear.

Caroline started feeding her family nutrient-dense food early on, and so did I. That's because we both believe in giving children a solid foundation when it comes to healthy living. This foundation lasts a lifetime and is the proverbial gift that keeps on giving. My college-aged son asked me to send him one of my cookbooks so he could make healthy food for himself and his roommates, and I am including a copy of this book as well because it belongs in every healthy household. It has a tremendous amount to offer readers both young and old. It's the answer to the daily question of "what's for dinner?" for every generation.

You need this book—and when you're standing in front of the fridge, deciding whether to make dinner or order takeout, you'll be thankful that you have it!

—Elana Amsterdam,
New York Times bestselling author and founder of Elana's Pantry

INTRODUCTION

Is there anyone who doesn't love an effortless, stress-free weeknight dinner? I enjoy a home-cooked meal as much as the next person, but even as a food blogger, I don't love spending all night every night hovering over the stove. I knew there had to be a way to combine healthy, delicious Paleo dishes with the best aspects of batch cooking and freezer meals, but I never found a method I loved . . . so I put on my apron and made my own. The Prep, Cook, Freeze method originated right in my kitchen, and now I'm sharing it with you!

What you're holding in your hands is the culmination of a ton of hard work and experimentation to create the very best meal planning method out there—and every single recipe is Paleo-friendly and packed with flavor. Using handy grocery lists and simple instructions, you will prep in one easy afternoon, so when dinner-time rolls around during the week, you can put a healthy, hearty meal on the table with minimal effort and hands-on time. And, because you're freezing elements from every meal, you're also prepping for *another* week's worth of dinners. If you're skeptical of freezer meals, don't be. When you're ready to reheat one meal—or an entire week of meals—you'll incorporate some key fresh ingredients, making them every bit as good as if you'd cooked them that same day. And there are grocery lists by meal for that, too!

Implementing this method in my own household has revolutionized our evenings; now, instead of cooking for hours when the kiddos get home from school, I meal prep with my husband, Chaz, on the weekends, freeing up our weeknights so we can spend time together as a family. What's more, there is *so* much less cleanup (which Chaz appreciates as my designated dish cleaner!). Even on our busiest evenings, there is always something we can grab from the freezer and have ready in 15 minutes.

Cooking has been one of my favorite hobbies since I was a little girl, and I've been creating recipes since before I could read or write. In elementary school, I would invite friends over and we would throw things together and see how they tasted. I would write out everything we did and instruct my mom to keep "the good ones." Fast-forward to when Chaz and I got married right after I graduated from the University of Georgia. I immediately got pregnant with our daughter, Ella, and when she was born at 30 weeks, I quickly had to figure out a job I could do from home. I decided to pursue my lifelong passion and started my blog Olive You Whole in 2014 to help others experience the life-changing benefits of the Paleo diet we followed. I wanted to create delicious recipes for my family and for others who were also living this lifestyle. My purpose has always been to help you live with vitality and longevity. Until now, I have fulfilled that mission with clean recipes and resources, but I wanted to give you something more.

I heard over and over again from Olive You Whole readers that you needed a way for weeknights to be easier. A system. And that's exactly what my Olive You Whole teammate Emily Steels and I are giving you with the Prep, Cook, Freeze method.

I'm sure you want effortless, stress-free weeknights just like I did. You want 15-minute meals that are healthy, delicious, filling and full of flavor. You want to prep once for 2 weeks of meals, and you want it *all* done for you in a way that's easy to follow. Well, here is your answer. We know that you'll love the Prep, Cook, Freeze method so much that you'll cook these meals over and over again for years to come.

Cheers to your health!
Caroline Fausel and Team Olive You Whole: Emily Steels

Caroline Fausel

AN OVERVIEW OF PREP, COOK, FREEZE

Prep, Cook, Freeze is a meal planning method that helps you get delicious, gourmet meals on the table faster. This method combines the best aspects of meal prepping, meal planning, batch cooking and freezer meals. On your prep day, you're actually making *2 weeks' worth* of meals. The prep-day instructions are all in one place, nestled together to make prep as efficient as possible. The ingredients and amounts are right next to the instructions, so there's no tedious flipping back and forth.

HERE'S AN OVERVIEW OF THE PROCESS:

Step 1: Shop for the week's ingredients using the provided grocery list. I include recommendations for Paleo-friendly brands in the grocery lists, as well as in the Paleo Pantry and Substitutions section (page 240).

Step 2: Designate a time to meal prep using the step-by-step instructions. You will batch cook and freeze an element from every meal. I like to do this prep on the weekend.

Step 3: Five nights a week, you will pull together a delicious dinner with very minimal hands-on time.

Step 4: Later, use the reheat grocery lists to make your frozen meals fresh. You can reheat the entire week of meals or choose to reheat them one at a time.

HOMEMADE OPTIONS

I integrated store-bought options whenever it could make your prep day and cook night even faster. If you'd like to go with the homemade options, use the notes provided and find all of the additional recipes in the Homemade Sauces, Dressings, Seasonings and Extras chapter (page 226).

FREEZING AND REHEATING TIPS

In almost every recipe, there are instructions to freeze a portion, if not all, of the meal you have prepared for reheat week. Here are some tips on how to freeze your food:

1. **Cool your food before freezing.** Give your food adequate time to cool before adding it to the freezer. Putting warm or even hot food into the freezer can warm up the temperature of the freezer as well as the items in it, which can affect the taste and texture of those other items. Additionally, the steam from a dish that's not cooled first will create ice when it freezes, and then water when it thaws. Also, do not crowd your freezer—allow for ample space to stack or lay items on top of one another.

2. **Freeze items in the proper containers.** Stasher bags and/or freezer-proof resealable bags are great, as you can squeeze the air out of them and lay them flat on top of one another. This method is especially great for sauces. Glass heatproof containers with lids are also great for freezing, so invest in a set. Be sure to leave space at the top when you are freezing liquids, as they will expand when freezing. If you need to use a storage container without a lid, I recommend first wrapping it in plastic wrap and then again in foil.

3. **Label and date.** Be sure to label and date every dish you make and freeze. You can write directly on a resealable bag or buy some painter's tape and a permanent marker to create your own labels. For reference, most cooked dishes last well for 2 to 3 months in the freezer.

4. **Thaw.** When you are ready for reheat week, be sure to allow adequate time when thawing your frozen portion of the meal. I recommend removing the frozen item the night before and allowing it to thaw in the refrigerator overnight.

HELPFUL HINTS:

- If you have leftover herbs that will go bad before you use them, make an herb oil by blending the herbs and olive oil in a blender and then freezing the herb oil in an ice cube tray. These are great to add to soups, stews, dressings and other recipes.

- Freeze your leftover broth, tomato paste, barbecue sauce and dressing in ice cube trays as well.

WEEK 1

I will make sure to say this just once: This is my favorite week in the entire cookbook. There are only a few lucky recipes in the book that have been previously published on my blog, and I just had to include my Chicken Tikka Masala recipe as one of them—it is the top reader favorite on the site. Meanwhile, the Thai Almond Noodle Bowls come together so quickly that you'll find yourself making them over and over. Chicken Fettuccine Alfredo was one of my very favorite dishes growing up, so the homemade version of this dairy-free Alfredo sauce (page 227) has been a game changer for me. And finally, these Sweet and Sour Hawaiian Meatballs are such a crowd-pleaser that they're my go-to meal to make for friends.

WEEK 1 PREP-DAY INSTRUCTIONS

This prep day is so easy, you're going to fly right through it! Using the pre-made tikka masala, sweet and sour and Alfredo sauces makes this week a breeze, though if you're feeling ambitious, you can whip up my homemade versions of these sauces (pages 228 and 227). You'll be making the Sweet and Sour Hawaiian Meatballs from scratch, and if you've never made homemade meatballs before, it's a skill you'll come to embrace thanks to how delicious they are.

Step 1:

CHICKEN TIKKA MASALA

2 (9.2-oz [272-ml]) jars tikka masala sauce

2 lbs (907 g) boneless, skinless chicken breasts, cut into 1-inch (2.5-cm) dice

Add the sauce to a gallon (4-L) plastic bag (or storage container of choice). Add the chicken and fully submerge it in the mixture. Seal or cover and chill for 1 hour in the refrigerator.

Step 2:

SWEET AND SOUR HAWAIIAN MEATBALLS

SWEET AND SOUR SAUCE

1 (9-oz [255-g]) jar Paleo-friendly island teriyaki sauce

1 (8.5-oz [241-g]) jar Paleo-friendly Hawaiian barbecue sauce

Juice from 1 (20-oz [566-g]) can pineapple chunks

MEATBALLS

2 lbs (907 g) ground pork

1 yellow onion, finely chopped

2 cloves garlic, minced

1 egg

2 tbsp (16 g) coconut flour

1 tsp ground ginger

½ tsp salt

¼ tsp black pepper

1 tbsp (15 ml) olive oil

While the chicken is marinating, make the sweet and sour sauce by blending together the jar of teriyaki sauce, jar of Hawaiian barbecue sauce and juice from the pineapple chunks in a high-powered blender.

Next, move on to the meatballs. In a large mixing bowl, fully combine all the meatball ingredients (except the olive oil), then mix them together with your hands. Line a sheet pan with parchment paper, then form golf ball–sized meatballs and place them on it.

Heat a large pot or Dutch oven over medium-high heat with the olive oil. Working in batches, cook the meatballs until they are browned on the outside and fully cooked through, 3 to 4 minutes per side, 6 to 8 minutes total. Drain the fat from the pot (which can be stored for later use or discarded). Add the meatballs back to the Dutch oven and pour the sweet and sour sauce over them. Simmer over medium heat until the sauce has thickened, about 10 minutes.

Once the sauce has thickened, remove the Dutch oven from the heat and allow the contents to cool completely. Divide the meatballs with their sauce mixture in half—store one half in an airtight container in the refrigerator for cook night and the other half in an airtight container in the freezer for reheat night.

Step 3:

TERIYAKI SLOPPY JOES WITH ASIAN SLAW

SLOPPY JOES

2 lbs (907 g) ground pork

2 large carrots, shredded

6 scallions, thinly sliced (white and green parts)

1 (9-oz [255-g]) jar Paleo-friendly teriyaki sauce

After you have stored your Hawaiian meatballs, it's time to prep the teriyaki-pork mixture. Heat a large sauté pan over medium-high, then brown the ground pork in it, heating until browned and cooked through, 5 to 7 minutes. Stir occasionally to break up the pork. Once cooked, add the carrots and sauté until soft, 5 to 7 minutes. Add the sliced scallions and sauté until fragrant, 1 to 2 minutes.

Add 1 cup (240 ml) of teriyaki sauce to the pork mixture. Stir to coat the pork and vegetables. Remove from the heat and allow to cool completely.

Step 4:

CHICKEN TIKKA MASALA

While the pork and vegetables cool, get out a large pot and pour the tikka masala sauce and marinated chicken from the bag into it.

Coat the chicken in the sauce, then simmer uncovered and undisturbed until the chicken is fully cooked and the sauce has thickened, 20 to 30 minutes.

Step 5:

CHICKEN FETTUCCINE ALFREDO WITH ROASTED BROCCOLI

2 lbs (907 g) boneless, skinless chicken breasts

2 tbsp (30 ml) olive oil

2 tsp (12 g) salt

1½ tsp (3 g) black pepper

While the chicken tikka masala is simmering, you'll cook the chicken for the chicken fettuccine Alfredo. To cook the chicken, heat a grill pan on the stovetop over medium-high heat. Brush the chicken breasts with olive oil and season on both sides with the salt and pepper. Once the grill pan is hot, place the chicken breasts in it and grill them on one side for 5 to 6 minutes, then turn them over and grill the other side for 5 to 6 minutes. Use an instant-read thermometer to check that the internal temperature of the chicken is 165°F (74°C), then remove them from the grill pan to rest and cool.

Step 6:

CHICKEN TIKKA MASALA

After you have cooked the chicken for the fettuccine Alfredo, the chicken in the simmering tikka masala should be fully cooked. Allow it to cool completely. Divide the chicken tikka masala into two equal portions. Store one portion in an airtight container in the refrigerator for cook night. Store the other half in an airtight container in the freezer for reheat night.

Step 7:

TERIYAKI SLOPPY JOES WITH ASIAN SLAW

After storing the chicken tikka masala, the teriyaki pork should be fully cooled. Divide it in half. Freeze one half of the mixture in the freezer for reheat night and store the other half in an airtight container in the refrigerator for cook night.

Step 8:

CHICKEN FETTUCCINE ALFREDO WITH ROASTED BROCCOLI

Next, it's time to store the chicken fettuccine Alfredo. Once the chicken is completely cooled, store half of the chicken breasts in an airtight container in the refrigerator for cook night and store the other half of the chicken breasts in an airtight container in the freezer for reheat night.

QUICK AND COLORFUL THAI ALMOND NOODLE BOWLS

Serves 4 on cook night and 4 on reheat night with the additional fresh ingredients found in the reheat grocery list on page 27

A variety of different peanut sauces are found in cultures all around the world, and this recipe is a Paleo take on the beloved and popular Thai peanut noodles. This is one of my very favorite Paleo meals because it is *packed* with veggies, and my kiddos still love it! Every time we make this, they ask when I can make it again. We even love this recipe for lunches—I will chop all of the produce and keep it in a mixing bowl covered with a damp cloth to keep it fresh, and it makes for a 5-minute lunch!

2 (8-oz [227-g]) boxes Paleo spaghetti or fettuccine noodles or 4 cups (600 g) spiralized vegetables

1 tbsp (15 ml) olive oil

1 (12-oz [340-g]) jar Paleo-friendly Thai almond sauce

1 (8-oz [227-g]) bag shredded red cabbage

1 (8-oz [227-g]) bag shredded carrots

1 red bell pepper, julienned

3 scallions, thinly sliced

⅓ cup (5 g) chopped cilantro

1 jalapeño, seeded and finely chopped (optional)

½ cup (54 g) sliced almonds

4 lime wedges

PREP DAY:

There's nothing to prep for this recipe because it comes together so quickly on cook night!

COOK NIGHT:

If you're using Paleo noodles, cook the noodles according to the package instructions. If you're using vegetable noodles, first spiralize them using your preferred method. In a large pot over medium-high heat, pour in the olive oil and cook until soft. Timing will depend on the type of vegetable you're using.

While the noodles are cooking, in a small pot on your stovetop, warm the Thai almond sauce over low heat, or heat it in the microwave on low for 30 seconds or until warm.

Plate the warm noodles. Top each individual serving with shredded cabbage and carrots, bell pepper, scallions, cilantro and jalapeño (if using). Pour the warm sauce over the vegetables and noodles, then garnish with sliced almonds and lime wedges.

REHEAT NIGHT:

Use your store-bought Paleo Thai almond sauce and follow the instructions for cook night.

NOTE: If you'd prefer to make the sauce from scratch, see page 227 for the Thai Almond Sauce recipe.

TERIYAKI SLOPPY JOES WITH ASIAN SLAW

Serves 4 on cook night and 4 on reheat night with the additional fresh ingredients found in the reheat grocery list on page 27

Did you eat sloppy joes as a kid? Me too. This recipe puts a fun Asian twist on the beloved classic sloppy joe. I usually use store-bought buns or lettuce cups to make this recipe faster, but let me tell you: If you have the time to spare, you *have* to try the homemade buns on page 226. After 6 years, I perfected Paleo pizza dough, and now I try to see how many different ways I can use it! You could use them as traditional yeast rolls, top them with ghee and garlic with your favorite Italian meal or top them with sesame seeds for burgers. AND they're freezable!

SLOPPY JOES

½ recipe teriyaki pork from the weekly prep (page 15)

1 package Paleo buns (store-bought or homemade, page 226) or 4 leaves Bibb lettuce, for lettuce cups

1 cucumber, sliced, for serving (optional)

ASIAN SLAW

1 (8-oz [227-g]) bag broccoli slaw

1 (8-oz [227-g]) bag shredded carrots

1 (11-oz [312-g]) can mandarin oranges, drained

¼ cup (27 g) sliced almonds, toasted

1 (8-oz [227-g]) jar Paleo-friendly sesame-ginger salad dressing

2 scallions, thinly sliced (white and green parts)

¼ cup (4 g) roughly chopped cilantro

PREP DAY:

See page 15 for the prep ingredients and instructions.

COOK NIGHT:

Reheat the teriyaki pork mixture in a sauté pan on the stovetop over medium-high heat for 5 minutes, or until warmed through.

To make the Asian slaw, in a large salad bowl, combine the broccoli slaw, shredded carrots, mandarin oranges and sliced almonds. Mix in the dressing and top with the sliced scallions and chopped cilantro.

Slice the buns in half. If you would like the buns warm, place them on a sheet pan in a 350°F (177°C) oven for 5 minutes before serving.

Spoon the pork mixture onto the bottom half of the buns and top with sliced cucumber (optional). Serve with a side of slaw.

REHEAT NIGHT:

In the morning, remove the teriyaki pork mixture from the freezer and leave at room temperature to thaw completely. Once the pork mixture is thawed, keep it in the refrigerator until ready to reheat. Thaw the buns overnight in the refrigerator or at room temperature day of. Separate the buns by hand or with a fork. Warm the buns on the broil setting until golden brown. Follow the instructions from cook night.

NOTE: If you'd prefer to make the buns and sauces from scratch, see page 226 for the Paleo Buns recipe, page 227 for the Asian Dressing recipe and page 226 for the Teriyaki Sauce recipe.

SWEET AND SOUR HAWAIIAN MEATBALLS

Serves 4 on cook night and 4 on reheat night with the additional fresh ingredients found in the reheat grocery list on page 27

These Hawaiian meatballs pack a serious punch. The flavor combinations will have you going back for more! We traveled to Hawaii a few years ago, and the delicious fresh pineapple there made me want to put it in every single recipe when we got back home. I'm a huge fan of the sweet and sour flavor combination, and this is it. You will love the onion, bell peppers and pineapples together!

SWEET AND SOUR SAUCE

1 tsp olive oil

1 bunch scallions, divided into white and green parts, thinly sliced

2 red bell peppers, ½-inch (1.3-cm) dice

Pineapple chunks from 1 (20-oz [566-g]) can pineapple chunks (juice separated and used during the weekly prep)

MEATBALLS

½ recipe sweet and sour meatballs from the weekly prep (page 14)

CAULIFLOWER RICE

1 tbsp (15 ml) olive oil

1 (16-oz [454-g]) bag frozen riced cauliflower

Salt, to taste

PREP DAY:

See page 14 for the prep ingredients and instructions.

COOK NIGHT:

In a large pot, heat the olive oil over medium-high heat. Add the white parts of the scallions and the chopped bell peppers and cook for 7 minutes, stirring occasionally. Add the drained pineapple chunks and cook until warmed through, about 5 minutes.

Remove the sweet and sour sauce base and Hawaiian meatballs from the refrigerator and add them to the same pot as the pineapple and bell peppers. Stir to combine and cook until heated through, about 8 minutes.

While that is cooking, make the cauliflower rice. In a different pan, heat the olive oil over medium-high heat. Add the frozen cauliflower rice and cook until it's warmed through, about 7 minutes. Add salt to taste.

Serve the cauliflower rice topped with the Hawaiian meatballs and sweet and sour sauce and sprinkle with the sliced green parts of the scallions.

REHEAT NIGHT:

To thaw the Hawaiian meatballs and sauce overnight, move them from the freezer to the refrigerator the night before reheat night. To thaw day of, move each container from the freezer to your countertop and allow the meatballs and sauce to completely thaw at room temperature. For a quick thaw, submerge each container in room temperature water until completely thawed. Once thawed, follow all of the cook night instructions.

NOTE: If you'd prefer to make the sauce from scratch, see page 228 for the Sweet and Sour Sauce recipe.

CHICKEN FETTUCCINE ALFREDO WITH ROASTED BROCCOLI

Serves 4 on cook night and 4 on reheat night with the additional fresh ingredients found in the reheat grocery list on page 27

Growing up, chicken fettuccine Alfredo was probably the dish I ordered the most eating out. What's more comforting than pasta and cheese sauce? It's recipes like these that I get most excited about making Paleo, because it seems impossible! My husband said this is even better than the real thing! I hope you think so, too.

½ recipe chicken for chicken fettuccine from the weekly prep (page 15)

1 (9-oz [255-g]) box Cappello's fettuccine noodles

1 head broccoli, cut into small florets

2 tbsp (30 ml) olive oil, divided

1 tsp salt

½ tsp black pepper

Pinch of red pepper flakes

1 (15.5-oz [440-g]) jar Paleo-friendly Alfredo sauce

1 tbsp (15 ml) freshly squeezed lemon juice

NOTE: If you'd prefer to make the sauce from scratch, see page 227 for the Alfredo Sauce recipe.

PREP DAY:

See page 15 for the prep ingredients and instructions.

COOK NIGHT:

Remove the grilled chicken from the refrigerator and preheat the oven to 400°F (204°C).

While the oven is preheating, bring a large pot of water to a boil on the stovetop and cook the Cappello's noodles according to the package directions.

While the noodles cook, spread the broccoli florets across a sheet pan and drizzle with 1 tablespoon (15 ml) of olive oil, the salt, black pepper and red pepper flakes. Toss to coat. Roast the broccoli in the oven for 15 minutes, flipping halfway through.

Meanwhile, heat 1 tablespoon (15 ml) of olive oil in a shallow skillet over medium heat, add the grilled chicken breasts and cook until heated through, 7 to 10 minutes.

Pour the Alfredo sauce into a saucepan over low heat and heat until warmed through, about 3 minutes.

Divide the cooked noodles between four plates and top them with the Alfredo sauce. Slice the chicken breasts on the diagonal and divide them evenly into four portions.

Remove the broccoli from the oven and drizzle with the lemon juice. Serve the roasted broccoli on the side.

REHEAT NIGHT:

To thaw the grilled chicken overnight, move the container from the freezer to the refrigerator the night before reheat night. To thaw day of, move the container from the freezer to your countertop and allow the chicken to completely thaw at room temperature. For a quick thaw, submerge the container in room temperature water until completely thawed. Once thawed, follow the instructions for cook night.

CHICKEN TIKKA MASALA

Serves 4 on cook night and 4 on reheat night with the additional fresh ingredients found in the reheat grocery list on page 27

It's hard for me to branch out at Indian restaurants, because I always know that chicken tikka masala will be amazing. Inevitably though, as good as it is, the heavy cream always gets me down, so years ago, I whipped up this Paleo version. Since that day, it has been the most-viewed recipe on my blog. It's a fan favorite, so I picked it as one of the *few* lucky blog recipes that made it into the cookbook. Now we can all quickly access it! It freezes and thaws beautifully for another meal with hardly any work.

½ recipe chicken for chicken tikka masala from the weekly prep (page 15)

1 tbsp (15 ml) olive oil

1 (12-oz [340-g]) bag frozen cauliflower rice

Salt, to taste

Chopped fresh cilantro, for garnish

NOTE: If you'd prefer to make Chicken Tikka Masala from scratch using a homemade sauce, see page 228 for the recipe.

PREP DAY:

See page 15 for the prep ingredients and instructions.

COOK NIGHT:

Remove the chicken tikka masala from the refrigerator. Reheat it in a large saucepan or Dutch oven over medium heat, stirring occasionally, until warmed through, 12 to 15 minutes.

Meanwhile, heat the olive oil in a sauté pan over medium-high heat. Add the frozen cauliflower rice and cook until warmed through, about 7 minutes. Add salt to taste.

Serve the chicken and sauce over the prepared cauliflower rice, and top with the chopped cilantro.

REHEAT NIGHT:

To thaw the chicken tikka masala overnight, move the container from the freezer to the refrigerator the night before reheat night. To thaw day of, move the container from the freezer to your countertop and allow the chicken tikka masala to completely thaw at room temperature. For a quick thaw, submerge the container in room temperature water until completely thawed. Once thawed, follow the instructions for cook night.

WEEK 1 GROCERY LIST

PROTEIN
- ☐ 4 lbs (1.8 kg) ground pork ● ●
- ☐ 1 egg ●
- ☐ 4 lbs (1.8 kg) boneless, skinless chicken breasts ● ●

PRODUCE
- ☐ 1 (8-oz [227-g]) bag shredded red cabbage ●
- ☐ 2 (8-oz [227-g]) bags shredded carrots ● ●
- ☐ 1 (12-oz [340-g]) bag broccoli slaw ●
- ☐ 3 red bell peppers ● ●
- ☐ 3 bunches scallions ● ● ●
- ☐ 2 bunches cilantro ● ● ● ●
- ☐ 1 jalapeño ●
- ☐ 1 lime ●
- ☐ 2 cloves garlic ●
- ☐ 2 large carrots ●
- ☐ 1 cucumber ●
- ☐ 2 yellow onions ●
- ☐ 1 head broccoli ●
- ☐ Lemon juice ●

SPICES
- ☐ Ground ginger ●
- ☐ Red pepper flakes ●

PANTRY
- ☐ ¾ cup (81 g) sliced almonds ● ●
- ☐ 2 (8-oz [227-g]) boxes Paleo noodles (I like Jovial Grain Free Cassava Spaghetti), or 4 cups (600 g) spiralized vegetables ●
- ☐ Coconut flour ●
- ☐ 1 (11-oz [312-g]) can mandarin oranges ●
- ☐ 1 (20-oz [566-g]) can pineapple chunks in juice ●
- ☐ 1 (8.5-oz [241-g]) jar Paleo-friendly teriyaki sauce (I like Primal Kitchen No Soy Teriyaki Sauce & Marinade) ●

- ☐ 1 (8-oz [237-ml]) jar Paleo-friendly Asian salad dressing (I like Primal Kitchen Sesame Ginger Vinaigrette & Marinade) ●
- ☐ 1 (12-oz [340-g]) jar Paleo-friendly Thai almond sauce (I like Yai's Thai Almond Sauce) ●
- ☐ 1 (15.5-oz [440-g]) jar Paleo-friendly Alfredo sauce (I like Primal Kitchen No-Dairy Alfredo Sauce) ●
- ☐ 1 (9-oz [255-g]) jar Paleo-friendly island teriyaki sauce (I like Primal Kitchen No Soy Island Teriyaki Sauce) ●
- ☐ 1 (8.5-oz [241-g]) jar Paleo-friendly Hawaiian barbecue sauce (I like Primal Kitchen Hawaiian Style BBQ Sauce) ●
- ☐ 2 (9.2-oz [272-ml]) jars Paleo-friendly tikka masala sauce (I like Good Food for Good Tikka Masala Cooking Sauce) ●

FREEZER
- ☐ 1 package frozen Paleo buns (I like Mikey's English Muffins) or 4 leaves of Bibb or comparable lettuce for lettuce cups ●
- ☐ 2 (12-oz [340-g]) bags frozen cauliflower rice ● ●
- ☐ 1 (9-oz [255-g]) box Cappello's fettuccine noodles ●

RECIPES KEY: ● ● ● ● ●

Sweet and Sour Hawaiian Meatballs (page 20)
Chicken Tikka Masala (page 24)
Chicken Fettuccini Alfredo with Roasted Broccoli (page 23)
Quick and Colorful Thai Almond Noodle Bowls (page 16)
Teriyaki Sloppy Joes with Asian Slaw (page 19)

WEEK 1 REHEAT GROCERY LIST

QUICK AND COLORFUL THAI ALMOND NOODLE BOWLS

- ☐ 2 (8-oz [227-g]) boxes Paleo noodles (I like Jovial Grain Free Cassava Spaghetti), or 4 cups (600 g) spiralized vegetables
- ☐ 1 (8-oz [227-g]) bag shredded red cabbage
- ☐ 1 (8-oz [227-g]) bag shredded carrots
- ☐ 1 red bell pepper
- ☐ 1 bunch scallions
- ☐ 1 bunch cilantro
- ☐ 1 jalapeño
- ☐ ½ cup (54 g) sliced almonds
- ☐ 1 lime
- ☐ 1 (12-oz [340-g]) jar Paleo-friendly Thai almond sauce (I like Yai's Thai Almond Sauce)

TERIYAKI SLOPPY JOES WITH ASIAN SLAW

- ☐ 1 package Paleo buns (I like Mikey's English Muffins) or 4 leaves of Bibb or comparable lettuce for lettuce cups

ASIAN SLAW

- ☐ 1 (12-oz [340-g]) bag broccoli slaw
- ☐ 1 (8-oz [227-g]) bag shredded carrots
- ☐ 1 (11-oz [312-g]) can mandarin oranges
- ☐ ¼ cup (27 g) sliced almonds
- ☐ 1 (8-oz [237-ml]) jar Paleo-friendly Asian salad dressing (I like Primal Kitchen Sesame Ginger Vinaigrette & Marinade)
- ☐ 1 bunch scallions
- ☐ 1 bunch cilantro
- ☐ 1 cucumber

SWEET AND SOUR HAWAIIAN MEATBALLS

- ☐ 1 bunch scallions
- ☐ 2 red bell peppers
- ☐ 1 (20-oz [566-g]) can pineapple chunks
- ☐ 1 (10-oz [283-g]) bag frozen cauliflower rice

CHICKEN FETTUCCINE ALFREDO WITH ROASTED BROCCOLI

- ☐ 1 (9-oz [255-g]) box Cappello's fettuccine noodles
- ☐ 1 head broccoli
- ☐ Red pepper flakes
- ☐ 1 (15.5-oz [440-g]) jar Paleo-friendly Alfredo sauce (I like Primal Kitchen No Dairy Alfredo)
- ☐ 1 lemon

CHICKEN TIKKA MASALA

- ☐ 1 (12-oz [340-g]) bag frozen cauliflower rice
- ☐ 1 bunch cilantro

WEEK 2

It's time to find your pastry chef hat! This week you'll be making a galette and the best-ever Paleo pizza dough if you'd like to make my homemade recipe (page 230). Don't fret—I've made both doughs simple and foolproof for you. The flavors of the samosa galette are divine, and you can make them into mini samosas if you're feeling ambitious! Week 2 features beef brisket and rotisserie chickens, and I absolutely love the ease of rotisserie chickens—you can even get already off-the-bone ones at some grocery stores.

WEEK 2 PREP-DAY INSTRUCTIONS

You're going to love this prep day because you only have to cook brisket once for two recipes! If you've never made a galette, you're in for a treat. Samosas are my favorite food at Indian restaurants, and turning them into a complete meal for the whole family is so much fun. You'll also be making my cashew-based charros beans—you would never know they're Paleo!

Step 1:

BARBECUE BEEF BRISKET WITH SOUTHERN COLLARD GREENS & BEEF BRISKET FAJITA SALAD WITH CILANTRO-LIME DRESSING

4 lbs (1.8 kg) beef brisket

3 tbsp (20 g) Paleo-friendly spice rub, homemade (page 229) or store-bought

2 tbsp (30 ml) olive oil

1 yellow onion, diced

3 cloves garlic, thinly sliced

1 cup (240 ml) beef or chicken bone broth

1 bay leaf

Make the brisket in an Instant Pot® for both recipes (or skip ahead for the stovetop instructions if you don't have an Instant Pot). Cut the brisket into four equal parts in order to fit into the Instant Pot and rub them with the Paleo-friendly spice rub.

Turn the Instant Pot to the sauté setting, pour in the olive oil and, working in batches, sear each piece of brisket, 3 to 4 minutes per side, until browned on all sides. Remove the beef and set aside.

Add the onion and garlic to the Instant Pot and sauté for 2 to 3 minutes, stirring constantly to release the browned bits. Then add the broth to deglaze the bottom of the pot.

Return the beef to the Instant Pot and add the bay leaf.

Set the Instant Pot to the Meat/Stew setting and cook for 60 minutes. Allow the steam to release naturally (this can take anywhere from 5 to 30 minutes).

If you do not have an Instant Pot, you can slow-roast the brisket in the oven on low heat for 3 to 4 hours depending on the size of the brisket. Preheat the oven to 300°F (149°C). Rub the brisket with the spice rub and place it in a large baking dish or roasting pan fat side up. In a large skillet or sauté pan, heat the olive oil over medium heat. Add the diced onion and sauté until translucent, 3 to 5 minutes. Add the garlic and sauté until fragrant. Add the bone broth and bay leaf, bring to a boil and then reduce to a simmer and simmer for 5 minutes. Remove the skillet from the heat and allow to cool slightly, then pour the liquid mixture over the brisket. Cover with foil or a lid and carefully place the brisket in the oven and bake for 4 hours until it's fall-apart tender. Remove the brisket from the oven and cool.

Step 2:

SAMOSA GALETTE WITH MINT CHUTNEY

SAMOSA FILLING

1 tbsp (6 g) plus 2 tsp (4 g) cumin

2½ tsp (4 g) coriander

2½ tsp (5 g) garam masala

2½ tsp (5 g) turmeric

3 tsp (18 g) salt

½ cup (120 g) unsalted ghee

4 russet potatoes, peeled and diced into ½-inch (1.3-cm) pieces

2 yellow onions, diced

6 carrots, diced into ½-inch (1.3-cm) pieces

1 cup (145 g) peas

2 cloves garlic, minced

1 (2-inch [5-cm]) piece ginger, minced (about ⅔ cup [90 g])

While the brisket is cooking, work on the samosa filling. To make the filling, put the cumin, coriander, garam masala, turmeric and salt in a small bowl and whisk to combine. Set aside.

In a large pot, melt the ghee over medium heat. Add the potatoes, onions, carrots and peas and sauté until the onions are translucent and the potatoes and carrots are tender, 5 to 7 minutes.

Add the garlic, ginger and spice mixture to the pot and stir to combine. Sauté for an additional 3 to 5 minutes, then remove from the heat and set aside.

GALETTE DOUGH

2 cups (250 g) cassava flour, divided

½ cup (51 g) almond flour, divided

¼ cup (31 g) coconut flour, divided

1 cup (128 g) tapioca starch, divided

½ tsp xanthan gum, divided

2 tsp (12 g) salt, divided

1 tsp turmeric, divided

1 tsp black pepper, divided

1 cup (240 g) unsalted ghee, cold, divided

6 egg yolks, divided

¾ cup (180 ml) ice water, divided

While the samosa veggies are cooking, make the galette dough. You'll be making this dough twice. (If you have an extra-large food processor, you may be able to fit the double batch in all at once.) In a food processor, add 1 cup (125 g) of cassava flour, ¼ cup (25 g) of almond flour, 2 tablespoons (16 g) of coconut flour, ½ cup (64 g) of tapioca starch, ¼ teaspoon of xanthan gum, 1 teaspoon of salt, ½ teaspoon of turmeric and ½ teaspoon of black pepper. Pulse in the food processor until well combined.

Add ½ cup (120 g) of cold ghee to the flour mixture and pulse until the texture looks like sand.

Add 3 egg yolks and 3 tablespoons (45 ml) of ice water and pulse until the mixture comes together and resembles a dough. Continue adding ice water, one teaspoon at a time, if the dough is too dry.

Remove the dough from the food processor and form it into a disc. Wrap the dough in plastic wrap and then aluminum foil and place in the freezer for reheat night.

Wash out the food processor and make a second batch of galette dough for cook night, wrap it in plastic wrap and foil and store in the refrigerator for cook night.

Once the samosa filling has completely cooled, divide the mixture into two equal portions and place both portions into airtight containers. Store one portion in the refrigerator for cook night and the other portion in the freezer for reheat night.

Step 3:

GREEN CHILE TACOS WITH CHARROS "BEANS" & BEST-EVER BARBECUE CHICKEN PIZZA

2 whole rotisserie chickens

Now that everything is complete for the samosa galettes, you'll move on to the green chile tacos. Shred the chicken off of the rotisserie chickens (you should get approximately 8 cups [1.1 kg] of chicken). Reserve 2½ cups (350 g) of chicken for the Best-Ever Barbecue Chicken Pizza and keep the remaining 5½ cups (770 g) of chicken for the green chile tacos.

Divide each portion (one for the pizza and the other for the tacos) of the chicken in half, storing one half in an airtight container in the refrigerator and the other half in an airtight container in the freezer.

Step 4:

BARBECUE BEEF BRISKET WITH SOUTHERN COLLARD GREENS & BEEF BRISKET FAJITA SALAD WITH CILANTRO-LIME DRESSING

After the brisket has cooked, place it on a cutting board and (once cool enough to handle) shred it using two forks.

Divide the shredded brisket into two portions (one for the barbecue and the other for the fajita salad).

Then divide each of the two portions in half for cook nights and reheat nights for each recipe. Store the cook-night portions in the refrigerator and the reheat-night portions in the freezer.

Step 5:

GREEN CHILE TACOS WITH CHARROS "BEANS"

CHARROS "BEANS"

8 strips bacon (from 1 [8-oz (226-g)] package)

1 yellow onion, ¼-inch (6-mm) dice (about 1 cup [160 g])

1 clove garlic, minced

1 jalapeño, seeded and chopped into ¼-inch (6-mm) dice

¾ tsp cumin

¾ tsp dried oregano

¾ tsp chili powder

3 cups (438 g) cashews

1½ cups (360 ml) beef bone broth

2 (14.5-oz [411-g]) cans fire-roasted diced tomatoes

2 (4-oz [113-g]) cans green chiles

Now that the brisket is cooked, divided and stored, it's time to make the charros beans. Chop the bacon into ½-inch (1.3-cm) pieces and place in a large skillet over medium heat. Cook, stirring, until the bacon is crispy, about 10 minutes. Add the onion and cook for an additional 5 minutes. Add the garlic, jalapeño, cumin, oregano and chili powder and cook until fragrant, about 1 minute more.

Add the cashews to the bacon-and-onion mixture and stir until coated.

Add the broth, diced tomatoes and green chiles. Bring the ingredients to a boil, then lower the heat to a simmer and cook, uncovered, until most of the liquid is absorbed, about 20 minutes.

Once the liquid is absorbed and the cashews are tender, remove the pan from the heat and let cool completely. Divide the charros beans into two equal portions. Store one portion in the refrigerator for cook night and the other portion in the freezer for reheat night.

SAMOSA GALETTE WITH MINT CHUTNEY

Serves 4 on cook night and 4 on reheat night with the additional fresh ingredients found in the reheat grocery list on page 45

We are huge fans of Indian food in our house. I could eat at an Indian lunch buffet every single day of the week. One of my favorite parts of an Indian meal is the beginning: kale pakoras, samosas, chutneys . . . there are so many appetizers and street foods to love, which inspired this samosa galette. It is an explosion of flavors and perfectly pairs with the mint chutney. I especially love that both the dough and filling can be made in advance, making it a fast but gourmet meal.

½ recipe samosa filling from the weekly prep (page 31)

½ recipe galette dough from the weekly prep (page 31)

MINT CHUTNEY

½ cup (8 g) fresh cilantro

½ cup (46 g) fresh mint leaves

¼ white onion

1 clove garlic

1 tsp fresh chopped ginger

1 tbsp (15 ml) lemon juice

½ tsp salt

½ tsp black pepper

1 tbsp (15 ml) water

PREP DAY:

See page 31 for the prep ingredients and instructions.

COOK NIGHT:

Preheat the oven to 375°F (191°C).

Remove the samosa filling and the galette dough from the refrigerator. Place the dough between two sheets of parchment paper or plastic wrap. Using a rolling pin, roll the dough out into a circle 12 inches (30 cm) wide and ¼ inch (6 mm) thick.

Line a sheet pan with parchment paper and move the galette dough to the sheet pan.

Spoon the samosa filling evenly onto the dough, leaving a 1-inch (2.5-cm) border along the edge. Make slits around the edge of the dough in even intervals. Fold the edge around the filling, creating a shingled effect.

Bake for 30 to 40 minutes, until the crust is golden brown around the edge.

While the galette is baking, make the mint chutney by placing all of the ingredients into a blender or food processor and blending until smooth. Pour into a bowl and set aside.

Cut the galette into fourths and serve with the mint chutney.

REHEAT NIGHT:

Move the samosa filling and galette dough from the freezer to the refrigerator the night before and allow time for both to thaw completely. Follow the instructions for cook night.

BARBECUE BEEF BRISKET WITH SOUTHERN COLLARD GREENS

Serves 4 on cook night and 4 on reheat night with the additional fresh ingredients found in the reheat grocery list on page 45

It doesn't get much better than barbecue beef brisket! Store-bought barbecue sauce gets the job done in this mouthwatering recipe, but I highly recommend taking the time to make my homemade version on page 229 because it is knock-your-socks-off good. I make this in huge batches to keep around for a quick meal. It pairs well with any protein, but *especially* with this beef brisket. A Southern barbecue isn't complete without collard greens!

SOUTHERN COLLARD GREENS

3 slices bacon, cut into small strips

1 shallot, thinly sliced

2 cloves garlic, thinly sliced

Pinch of red pepper flakes

2 bunches collard greens, ribs removed and roughly chopped

½ cup (120 ml) chicken bone broth

1 tbsp (15 ml) coconut aminos

1 tbsp (15 ml) apple cider vinegar

Salt and pepper, to taste

¼ recipe beef brisket from the weekly prep (page 30)

1 (8.5-oz [241-g]) jar Paleo-friendly barbecue sauce

PREP DAY:

See page 30 for the prep ingredients and instructions.

COOK NIGHT:

Make the collard greens in a large pot on the stovetop. Begin by putting the bacon strips in the pot and cooking over medium-high heat until the fat is rendered and the bacon is crispy, 3 to 5 minutes. Remove the bacon strips from the pot and add the shallot, garlic and pinch of red pepper flakes to the bacon fat. Sauté until the shallot is translucent and the garlic is fragrant, 2 to 3 minutes.

Add the collard greens to the pot and sauté until they begin to wilt and become tender, 3 to 5 minutes. Add the chicken bone broth, coconut aminos, apple cider vinegar and salt and pepper to taste. Stir to combine, then cover the pot and simmer on low for 15 minutes.

Remove the brisket from the refrigerator and reheat in a pot on the stovetop over medium heat. Add ½ to 1 cup (120 to 240 ml) of barbecue sauce to the brisket and stir to combine, and continue to cook until heated through.

Serve the brisket with the collard greens.

REHEAT NIGHT:

To thaw the day of, remove the container from the freezer and allow the brisket to completely thaw at room temperature. For a quick thaw, submerge the container in room temperature water until completely thawed. Once thawed, follow the instructions for cook night.

NOTE: If you'd prefer to make the spice rub and barbecue sauce from scratch, see page 229 for the Spice Rub recipe and page 229 for the Barbecue Sauce recipe.

BEEF BRISKET FAJITA SALAD WITH CILANTRO-LIME DRESSING

Serves 4 on cook night and 4 on reheat night with the additional fresh ingredients found in the reheat grocery list on page 45

Y'all know I could eat Mexican food all day every day. (Which is why our honeymoon in Mexico was the *perfect* destination! Good call, Chaz!) Fajitas are an easy Paleo choice because they're just meat and veggies, and this recipe makes them even easier by turning them into a salad. This cilantro-lime dressing will become a favorite!

¼ beef brisket recipe (see prep day notes, page 30)

2 tbsp (30 ml) olive oil

1 yellow onion, thinly sliced

1 red bell pepper, seeded and thinly sliced

1 orange bell pepper, seeded and thinly sliced

1 yellow bell pepper, seeded and thinly sliced

Salt and pepper, to taste

2 avocados

2 heads romaine lettuce

1 (8-oz [237-ml]) jar Paleo-friendly cilantro-lime dressing

PREP DAY:

See page 30 for the prep ingredients and instructions.

COOK NIGHT:

Remove the beef brisket from the refrigerator. In a large skillet or cast-iron pan, heat the oil over medium-high heat. Add the sliced onion and bell peppers and sauté until they are tender and begin to char, 8 to 10 minutes. Season to taste with salt and pepper. Remove from the pan and set aside.

While the onion and bell peppers are cooking, slice the avocados and set aside.

Using the same pan, put in the beef brisket and sauté until warmed through. While the brisket is heating, wash the lettuce and cut both heads into 1-inch (2.5-cm) slices. Remove the brisket and bell peppers from the heat and set aside.

Build your salads by layering a bed of lettuce, sautéed onion and bell peppers, beef brisket and sliced avocado, and top with the cilantro-lime dressing.

REHEAT NIGHT:

To thaw the day of, remove the container from the freezer and allow the brisket to completely thaw at room temperature. For a quick thaw, submerge the container in room temperature water until completely thawed. Once thawed, follow the instructions for cook night.

NOTE: If you'd prefer to make the Cilantro-Lime Dressing from scratch, see page 229.

GREEN CHILE TACOS WITH CHARROS "BEANS"

Serves 4 on cook night and 4 on reheat night with the additional fresh ingredients found in the reheat grocery list on page 45

One of the things that became more prominent in my life with our move to Colorado is green chiles. Green chiles are actually called "New Mexico Chiles" because they were first grown in New Mexico. Because of our proximity, we have the privilege of enjoying green chiles in a slew of different dishes. We can even get freshly roasted green chiles in the summer! Enjoy these tacos with these unique charros "beans"—you will be so surprised they are actually cashews!

½ recipe (about 2¾ cups [385 g]) shredded rotisserie chicken from the weekly prep (page 33)

½ recipe charros "beans" from the weekly prep (page 33)

1 (15-oz [425-g]) jar Paleo-friendly green chile sauce

Avocado, for garnish (optional)

Radish, sliced, for garnish (optional)

Lime wedge, for garnish (optional)

1 (8-piece) package grain-free tortillas

PREP DAY:

See page 33 for the prep ingredients and instructions.

COOK NIGHT:

Remove the shredded chicken and charros "beans" from the refrigerator.

Put the green chile sauce and the shredded chicken in a large pot or Dutch oven over medium heat and heat until warmed through.

Put the charros "beans" in a separate saucepan and add water or broth if necessary for the desired texture. Reheat over medium heat until warmed through.

Meanwhile, prepare the optional garnishes for your tacos and heat up your tortillas according to the package instructions.

Build your tacos and serve with the charros "beans."

REHEAT NIGHT:

To thaw the charros "beans" and shredded chicken overnight, move them from the freezer to the refrigerator the night before reheat night. To thaw day of, move each container from the freezer to your countertop and allow the beans and chicken to completely thaw at room temperature. For a quick thaw, submerge each container in room temperature water until completely thawed. Once thawed, follow all of the instructions for cook night.

NOTE: If you'd prefer to make the sauce from scratch, see page 229 for the Green Chile Sauce recipe.

BEST-EVER BARBECUE CHICKEN PIZZA

Serves 4 on cook night and 4 on reheat night with the additional fresh ingredients found in the reheat grocery list on page 45

Who says you can't have pizza on the Paleo diet? This is one of my very favorite pizzas, and the barbecue sauce really takes it up a notch. Using a store-bought crust speeds things up for your busiest nights, but when you have the time, be sure to make the Paleo pizza dough on page 230 that took me 7 years to master! I can't even put into words my excitement when I finally came up with a Paleo pizza dough that's egg free, nut free and *yeasted.* It's really one of a kind. And what better way to show it off than with a barbecue chicken pizza? It's one of my very favorite pizzas, and my homemade barbecue sauce (page 229) takes it up a notch if you'd like to try it!

¼ cup (40 g) thinly sliced red onion

½ cup (83 g) pineapple chunks

1 cup (112 g) vegan mozzarella cheese, shredded

1 (8.5-oz [241-g]) jar Paleo-friendly barbecue sauce, divided

1 portion (1¼ cups [175 g]) shredded rotisserie chicken from the weekly prep (page 33)

1 Paleo-friendly pre-made pizza crust

1 tbsp (15 ml) olive oil

2 tbsp (2 g) roughly chopped cilantro

PREP DAY:

See page 33 for the prep ingredients and instructions.

COOK NIGHT:

Preheat the oven to 425°F (218°C).

While the oven heats, prepare your pizza toppings: the onion, pineapple and vegan mozzarella. Combine ½ cup (120 ml) of barbecue sauce with the shredded chicken.

Place your pizza crust on a parchment-lined baking sheet or pizza stone. Lightly brush your pizza crust with olive oil.

Spread ⅓ cup (80 ml) of straight barbecue sauce onto the pizza dough, then top with the mozzarella cheese, barbecue shredded chicken, red onion and pineapple.

Place the pizza in the oven and bake for 7 to 10 minutes, until the cheese has melted and the crust is fully cooked.

Garnish with chopped cilantro and serve.

REHEAT NIGHT:

To thaw the shredded chicken overnight, move it from the freezer to the refrigerator the night before reheat night. To thaw day of, move the container from the freezer to your countertop and allow the chicken to completely thaw at room temperature. For a quick thaw, submerge the container in room temperature water until completely thawed. Once thawed, follow all of the instructions for cook night.

NOTE: If you'd prefer to make the pizza dough and the barbecue sauce from scratch, see page 230 for the Pizza Dough recipe and page 229 for the Barbecue Sauce recipe.

WEEK 2 GROCERY LIST

PROTEIN
- ☐ 6 eggs ●
- ☐ 4 lbs (1.8 kg) beef brisket ● ●
- ☐ 2 (8-oz [226-g]) packages Paleo-friendly bacon ● ●
- ☐ 2 whole rotisserie chickens ● ●

PRODUCE
- ☐ 4 russet potatoes ●
- ☐ 5 yellow onions ● ● ● ●
- ☐ 1 white onion ●
- ☐ 6 carrots ●
- ☐ 1 head garlic ● ● ● ●
- ☐ 1 (3-inch [7.5-cm]) piece fresh ginger ●
- ☐ 2 bunches collard greens ●
- ☐ 1 shallot ●
- ☐ 1 jalapeño ●
- ☐ Lemon juice ●
- ☐ 2 bunches cilantro ● ●
- ☐ 1 bunch mint ●
- ☐ 1 red onion ●
- ☐ 1 red bell pepper ●
- ☐ 1 orange bell pepper ●
- ☐ 1 yellow bell pepper ●
- ☐ 2 heads romaine lettuce ●
- ☐ 2 avocados plus 1 for garnish (optional) ● ●
- ☐ Radish, for garnish (optional) ●
- ☐ 1 lime, for garnish (optional) ●

SPICES
- ☐ Cumin ● ●
- ☐ Coriander ●
- ☐ Garam masala ●
- ☐ Turmeric ●
- ☐ Chili powder ●
- ☐ Bay leaf ● ●
- ☐ Red pepper flakes ●
- ☐ Dried oregano ●

PANTRY
- ☐ Cassava flour ●
- ☐ Almond flour ●
- ☐ Coconut flour ●
- ☐ Tapioca starch ●
- ☐ Xanthan gum ●
- ☐ 1 (32-oz [960-ml]) box beef bone broth ● ● ●
- ☐ Coconut aminos ●
- ☐ 1 (32-oz [960-ml]) box chicken bone broth ●
- ☐ Apple cider vinegar ●
- ☐ 3 cups (438 g) cashews (raw) ●
- ☐ 2 (14.5-oz [411-g]) cans diced tomatoes, fire roasted ●
- ☐ 2 (4-oz [113-g]) cans green chiles ●
- ☐ 1 (14-oz [400-g]) can pineapple chunks ●
- ☐ 3 tbsp (32 g) Paleo-friendly barbecue spice rub (I like Primal Palate Barbecue Rub) ● ●
- ☐ 2 (8.5-oz [241-g]) jars Paleo-friendly BBQ sauce (I like Primal Kitchen Classic BBQ Sauce) ● ●
- ☐ 1 (15-oz [425-g]) jar Paleo-friendly green chile sauce (I like Siete Green Enchilada Sauce) ●
- ☐ 1 (8-oz [237-ml]) jar Paleo-friendly cilantro-lime dressing (I like Primal Kitchen Cilantro Lime Dressing and Marinade) ●

DAIRY ALTERNATIVES
- ☐ 1½ cups (360 g) unsalted ghee (I like Fourth & Heart) ●
- ☐ 1 cup (112 g) vegan mozzarella cheese (I like Miyoko's) ●

FREEZER
- ☐ 1 (8-piece) package taco-sized grain-free tortillas (I like Siete Cassava Tortillas) ●
- ☐ 1 cup (145 g) frozen peas ●
- ☐ 1 Paleo-friendly frozen pre-made pizza crust (I like Cappello's Naked Pizza Crust) ●

RECIPES KEY: ● ● ● ● ●

WEEK 2 REHEAT GROCERY LIST

SAMOSA GALETTE WITH MINT CHUTNEY

- ☐ 1 bunch cilantro
- ☐ 1 bunch mint
- ☐ 1 white onion
- ☐ 1 head garlic
- ☐ 1 (1-inch [2.5-cm]) piece fresh ginger
- ☐ Lemon juice

BARBECUE BEEF BRISKET WITH SOUTHERN COLLARD GREENS

- ☐ 2 bunches collard greens
- ☐ 1 (8-oz [226-g]) package Paleo-friendly bacon
- ☐ 1 shallot
- ☐ 2 cloves garlic
- ☐ Red pepper flakes
- ☐ 1 (32-oz [960-ml]) box chicken bone broth
- ☐ Coconut aminos
- ☐ Apple cider vinegar
- ☐ 1 (8.5-oz [241-g]) jar Paleo-friendly barbecue sauce (I like Primal Kitchen Classic BBQ Sauce)

BEEF BRISKET FAJITA SALAD WITH CILANTRO-LIME DRESSING

- ☐ 1 yellow onion
- ☐ 1 red bell pepper
- ☐ 1 orange bell pepper
- ☐ 1 yellow bell pepper
- ☐ 2 heads romaine lettuce
- ☐ 2 avocados
- ☐ 1 (8-oz [237-ml]) jar Paleo-friendly cilantro-lime dressing (I like Primal Kitchen Cilantro Lime Dressing and Marinade)

GREEN CHILE TACOS WITH CHARROS "BEANS"

- ☐ 1 (8-piece) package taco-sized grain-free tortillas (I like Siete Cassava Tortillas)
- ☐ Avocado, for garnish (optional)
- ☐ Radish, for garnish (optional)
- ☐ 1 lime, for garnish (optional)
- ☐ 1 (15-oz [425-g]) jar Paleo-friendly green chile sauce (I like Siete Green Enchilada Sauce)

BEST-EVER BARBECUE CHICKEN PIZZA

- ☐ 1 red onion
- ☐ 1 (20-oz [566-g]) can pineapple chunks
- ☐ 1 (8-oz [226-g]) package Miyoko's vegan mozzarella cheese
- ☐ 1 bunch cilantro
- ☐ 1 Paleo-friendly pre-made pizza crust (I like Cappello's Naked Pizza Crust)
- ☐ 1 (8.5-oz [241-g]) jar Paleo-friendly BBQ sauce (I like Primal Kitchen Classic BBQ Sauce)

WEEK 3

You will *love* the ease of this week, which features two fully frozen meals—my favorite kind because they're such a breeze to thaw and have dinner on the table with nearly zero hands-on time! I love diversifying my proteins, and the turkey featured this week is a great way to do that. This week is also filled with Mediterranean flavors with the Spanish romesco sauce, the Greek salmon salad with potato salad and the Mediterranean quiche. This is the perfect week when you are at your busiest because, in addition to the completely done meals I mentioned, the salmon cooks quickly.

WEEK 3 PREP-DAY INSTRUCTIONS

There are so many different techniques in today's prep day. You can do it! So many of these meals can be entirely frozen, making today's prep day even more worth it. Not-Your-Mom's Turkey Tetrazzini is a family favorite. You'll even get some breakfast for dinner with the Mediterannean quiche. The Southern Cranberry-Pecan Turkey Salad is going to give you all of the Thanksgiving vibes. You'll end your prep day with an easy Sheet Pan Romesco Salmon with Patatas Bravas that was one of my recipe testers' biggest family favorites.

Step 1:

NOT-YOUR-MOM'S TURKEY TETRAZZINI

2 (9-oz [255-g]) packages Paleo fettuccine noodles

If you're using Cappello's fettuccine noodles, remove both packages from the freezer and let them come to room temperature (not necessary if you're using dried noodles).

Step 2:

MEDITERRANEAN QUICHE

QUICHE CRUST

2 cups (250 g) cassava flour

½ cup (51 g) almond flour

¼ cup (31 g) coconut flour

1 cup (128 g) tapioca starch

½ tsp xanthan gum

2 tsp (12 g) salt

1 cup (227 g) unsalted ghee, cold

6 egg yolks

¾ cup (180 ml) ice water

While the fettuccini noodles are thawing, make the crusts for the two quiches. First, preheat your oven to 350°F (177°C).

Combine the dry ingredients in a food processor and pulse a few times until combined. Add the ghee to the flours in the food processor, and pulse until the ghee is about the size of small peas and the dough looks shaggy.

Add the egg yolks one at a time and pulse a few times between each until the eggs are incorporated. With the food processor running, add the ice water, 1 tablespoon (15 ml) at a time, until the dough forms one big ball in your food processor. You may not need to use it all depending on the size of the egg yolks. Divide the dough into two halves, and roll each into balls.

Cut four sheets of wax paper into 13-inch (33-cm) squares. Place two sheets side by side, wax side up. Place the balls of dough into the center of each of the two squares. Place the other two sheets of wax paper wax side down onto each ball of dough.

Using a rolling pin on the top wax paper, roll one ball of dough into a 13-inch (33-cm) circle, about ⅛ inch (3 mm) thick. Remove one top sheet of wax paper, then turn over the rolled dough and place it directly in the center of a standard 9-inch (23-cm) pie pan. Repeat this process for the second dough ball. Peel back the bottom pieces of wax paper. Slowly press each piece of dough into its respective pie pan, pressing the sides down and then the top. Use a pizza cutter or sharp knife to remove any extra dough hanging around the edges of the pie pans. Crimp the dough along the edges of the pie pan and, using a fork, poke the bottom of the crust a few times.

You will blind bake the crusts (which means to bake the crust without the filling) first in the preheated oven for 20 minutes.

QUICHE FILLING

¼ cup (60 ml) olive oil

4 shallots, finely chopped

4 cloves garlic, minced

¼ tsp red pepper flakes

2 cups (440 g) quartered marinated artichoke hearts, roughly chopped

½ cup (27 g) sun-dried tomatoes, drained and chopped

8 cups (1 [5-oz (141-g)] package) baby spinach

12 eggs

1½ cups (360 ml) almond or coconut milk, unsweetened

1 tsp salt

1 tsp black pepper

½ cup (12 g) basil leaves, chopped

While the pie crusts are blind baking, make the quiche filling. In a large skillet, heat the olive oil over medium heat. Add the chopped shallots and sauté until they are translucent, about 5 minutes. Add the minced garlic and red pepper flakes and sauté until fragrant, about 1 minute more. Add the artichoke hearts and sun-dried tomatoes. Stir to combine and heat through, 2 to 3 minutes.

Add the baby spinach and sauté until wilted, 3 to 5 minutes. Stir this vegetable mixture to combine and set it aside to cool, about 10 minutes.

While the vegetable mixture is cooling, in a large bowl, combine the eggs, nut milk, salt and pepper and whisk together. Once the vegetable mixture has cooled, add it to the egg mixture with the chopped basil and stir to combine.

Remove the two pie crusts from the oven, but keep the oven at 350°F (177°C). Pour half of the quiche mixture into the first pie crust, and the remaining half into the second pie crust, ensuring that the distribution of veggies and eggs is even between the two quiches. Bake both quiches in the oven for 30 to 35 minutes, or until they are set and golden brown.

Step 3:

NOT-YOUR-MOM'S TURKEY TETRAZZINI & SOUTHERN CRANBERRY-PECAN TURKEY SALAD

NOTE: *The 4 lbs (1.8 kg) of turkey breast is for two full recipes plus reheat weeks. If only making for one recipe at a time, divide the herbed turkey breast in half.*

1 cup (240 ml) chicken bone broth

2 tsp (6 g) herbs de Provence

1 tsp salt

1 tsp black pepper

1 tbsp (15 ml) olive oil

4 lbs (1.8 kg) turkey breast (see Note)

1 small onion, sliced

1 stalk celery, cut into 1-inch (2.5-cm) pieces

2 cloves garlic, smashed

While the quiches are baking, you will cook the turkey breast for both turkey recipes in your Instant Pot (if you don't have an Instant Pot, skip ahead for the stovetop instructions). Place the trivet at the bottom of the Instant Pot and pour in the chicken bone broth.

In a small bowl, mix together the herbs, salt, pepper and olive oil. Rub the herb mixture all over the turkey breast and place the breast into the Instant Pot. Place the onion, celery and garlic around the turkey breast. Seal the Instant Pot and press Manual, High Pressure and set the timer for 30 minutes.

(continued)

If you do not have an Instant Pot, preheat your oven to 325°F (163°C). Place the turkey breast skin side up on a rack in a roasting pan or in a large baking dish. Drizzle the turkey with the olive oil, then sprinkle the herbs, salt and pepper all over the turkey breast. Pour the chicken broth in the bottom of the pan and add the garlic cloves, onion and celery. Roast the turkey breast for 1½ hours (approximately 20 minutes per pound [454 g]) and, using a meat thermometer, check that the internal temperature is 165°F (74°C). Once the turkey is cooked, remove it from the oven, tent it with foil and let it sit for 15 to 20 minutes.

Step 4:

SHEET PAN ROMESCO SALMON WITH PATATAS BRAVAS & GREEK SALMON SALAD WITH HERBY POTATO SALAD

While the turkey is cooking, bring salted water to a boil in two separate large pots for the patatas bravas and the potato salad.

Step 5:

MEDITERRANEAN QUICHE

Once the quiches are done baking, remove them from the oven. Insert a knife 1 inch (2.5 cm) into the center of the quiche; if the knife is clean when removed, then the quiche is done. If not, return the quiche to the oven for a few more minutes. Once cooked through, allow both quiches to fully cool. Once cooled, tightly cover both of the quiches with plastic wrap, then also wrap them in aluminum foil. Put one in the refrigerator and one in the freezer.

Step 6:

SHEET PAN ROMESCO SALMON WITH PATATAS BRAVAS & GREEK SALMON SALAD WITH HERBY POTATO SALAD

3 lbs (1.4 kg) russet potatoes, chopped into 1-inch (2.5-cm) cubes

2 lbs (907 g) red potatoes, chopped into large pieces

Once the quiches are baked, cooled and stored, the water should be boiling. Add the russet potatoes to one pot and cook for 5 minutes. Add the red potatoes to the other pot and cook for 10 to 15 minutes. When each of the potatoes are done, drain the potatoes, spray with cold water, dry using a kitchen towel and store in the refrigerator until cook night.

Step 7:

NOT-YOUR-MOM'S TURKEY TETRAZZINI & SOUTHERN CRANBERRY-PECAN TURKEY SALAD

Once the potatoes are cooked and stored, the turkey should be done cooking. If you used the Instant Pot, allow it to naturally release for 15 minutes. Release the vent, carefully open the Instant Pot and remove the turkey breast.

Once the turkey is cool enough to handle, shred the turkey using forks or using the whisk attachment on your stand mixer.

Set aside 3 cups (420 g) of the shredded turkey to be used in the tetrazzini. Divide the remaining shredded turkey into two equal portions. Set one portion aside to continue with the cranberry-pecan turkey salad recipe. Freeze the other portion in an airtight container for reheat night.

Step 8:

SOUTHERN CRANBERRY-PECAN TURKEY SALAD

¾ cup (180 ml) Paleo-friendly mayonnaise

2 tbsp (30 ml) maple syrup

½ tsp salt

½ tsp black pepper

½ cup (61 g) dried cranberries

½ cup (55 g) pecans, rough chopped

⅓ cup (34 g) diced celery

¼ cup (40 g) diced red onion

Now that your turkey is cooked, cooled and shredded, you can make the Southern Cranberry-Pecan Turkey Salad. In a large mixing bowl, combine the mayonnaise with the maple syrup, salt and pepper. Add the shredded turkey breast, cranberries, pecans, celery and red onion and stir until all of the ingredients are fully coated.

Store the turkey salad in an airtight container until cook night.

Step 9:

NOT-YOUR-MOM'S TURKEY TETRAZZINI

2 tbsp (28 g) unsalted ghee

1 (8-oz [226-g]) container sliced baby bella mushrooms

1 green bell pepper, ¼-inch (6-mm) dice

1 red bell pepper, ¼-inch (6-mm) dice

1 cup (134 g) frozen peas

1 (4-oz [113-g]) jar pimientos, drained

2 tsp (1 g) chopped fresh thyme

1 tsp dried oregano

1 tsp salt

1 tsp black pepper

3 cups (420 g) cooked turkey breast, shredded

2 (15.5-oz [440-g]) jars Paleo-friendly Alfredo sauce

½ cup (120 ml) chicken broth

1 cup (56 g) Paleo bread crumbs, divided

Once you're done with the turkey salad, in a large skillet or sauté pan, heat the ghee over medium-high heat. Add the mushrooms and sauté until they are tender, about 5 minutes. Add the diced green and red bell peppers and sauté for an additional 5 minutes. Add the peas, pimientos, thyme, oregano, salt and pepper, then stir to combine. Remove this mixture from the heat.

To this vegetable mixture, add the shredded turkey, jars of Paleo-friendly Alfredo sauce and the chicken broth and stir to combine.

Spray two 8 x 8-inch (20 x 20-cm) baking dishes with avocado oil cooking spray.

Add 1 package of Cappello's fettuccine noodles from step 1 to each baking dish and spread the noodles apart, loosely covering the bottom of each baking dish. Divide the sauce and vegetable mixture in half and pour each half into a baking dish, covering the noodles. Divide the bread crumbs into two equal portions and sprinkle on top of each dish.

Let both casseroles completely cool, then wrap them first in plastic wrap, then in foil. Keep one in the refrigerator for cook night and one in the freezer for reheat night.

SOUTHERN CRANBERRY-PECAN TURKEY SALAD

Serves 4 on cook night and 4 on reheat night with the additional fresh ingredients found in the reheat grocery list on page 63

Turkey reminds a lot of us of Thanksgiving, which is the inspiration for this fast-and-easy recipe. The flavors of maple syrup, cranberries, pecans and celery all come from a delicious Thanksgiving meal. I prep a lot of this turkey salad and use it for quick lunches—either salads or sandwiches. You can also replace the turkey breast with chicken breast if you prefer.

½ recipe Southern cranberry-pecan turkey salad from the weekly prep (page 49)

2 heads romaine lettuce

PREP DAY:

See page 49 for the prep ingredients and instructions.

COOK NIGHT:

Remove the turkey salad from the refrigerator. Chop the romaine lettuce into 1-inch (2.5-cm) pieces. On each plate, serve the turkey salad on a bed of lettuce.

REHEAT NIGHT:

To thaw the turkey overnight, move it from the freezer to the refrigerator the night before reheat night. To thaw day of, move the container from the freezer to your countertop and allow the turkey to completely thaw at room temperature. For a quick thaw, submerge the container in room temperature water until completely thawed. Once thawed, follow the instructions on prep day to make the turkey salad. Follow the instructions on cook night to serve.

SHEET PAN ROMESCO SALMON WITH PATATAS BRAVAS

Serves 4 on cook night and 4 on reheat night with the additional fresh ingredients found in the reheat grocery list on page 63

Have you ever had romesco sauce? It's one of those sauces that I could put on just about everything. Romesco is a sauce that originated in northeast Spain. It is typically made with tomatoes, garlic, peppers, almonds and olive oil. See why it's so delicious? It pairs well with this salmon, and when I make this meal, I use it as a sauce for the patatas bravas, too. These patatas bravas are *so* crispy and delicious. When paired with romesco sauce, they're also a great tapa for parties.

PATATAS BRAVAS

1 recipe par-boiled russet potatoes from the weekly prep (page 50)

¼ cup (60 ml) olive oil

½ tsp smoked paprika

Salt and pepper, to taste

ROMESCO SALMON

1 lb (454 g) salmon, cut into 4 fillets

1 (12-oz [340-g]) jar Paleo-friendly romesco sauce

PREP DAY:

See page 50 for the prep ingredients and instructions.

COOK NIGHT:

Arrange your oven's racks on the top and bottom third of the oven, then preheat the oven to 400°F (204°C).

Take the potatoes out of the refrigerator and toss in the olive oil, paprika, salt, and pepper until they are well coated. Spread across a baking sheet and place in the oven. Bake the potatoes for 20 minutes.

While the potatoes are cooking, line a baking sheet with parchment paper or foil and put the salmon fillets on it, skin side down. Spoon ½ cup (120 ml) of romesco sauce over the fillets. After the potatoes have cooked for 10 minutes, remove them from the oven to stir, then place them back in the oven. Also at this time, add your salmon to another rack and bake it for 10 minutes, or until the salmon is flaking around the edges. Remove the salmon from the oven.

Turn the oven to broil and cook the potatoes for another 3 minutes, or until they have gotten nice and crispy. Remove the potatoes from the oven.

Serve the salmon with the patatas bravas, plus additional romesco sauce for dipping the salmon and the potatoes.

REHEAT NIGHT:

Boil the potatoes using the instructions from prep day.

Bake the potatoes and salmon using the instructions from cook night.

> **NOTE:** If you'd prefer to make the sauce from scratch, see page 230 for the Romesco Sauce recipe.

NOT-YOUR-MOM'S TURKEY TETRAZZINI

Serves 4 on cook night and 4 on reheat night with the additional fresh ingredients found in the reheat grocery list on page 63

This recipe brings me so much joy because it was one of my mom's staples when I was growing up. This dish apparently originated in San Francisco and was named after the opera singer Luisa Tetrazzini. I honestly have no idea how it got into my mom's kitchen in Nashville, but I'm glad it did! The original version packs in the gluten and dairy, so you'll love this cleaned-up Paleo version. Tip: You can replace the turkey breast with chicken breast.

½ recipe turkey tetrazzini from the weekly prep (page 48)

Parsley, chopped, for garnish (optional)

PREP DAY:

See page 48 for the prep ingredients and instructions.

COOK NIGHT:

Remove the casserole from the refrigerator 30 minutes before warming. Remove the plastic wrap and aluminum foil.

Preheat the oven to 350°F (177°C).

Once the casserole is at room temperature, place it in the oven and cook for 30 to 40 minutes, or until warmed through. Garnish with chopped parsley (optional), slice into fourths and serve.

REHEAT NIGHT:

Move the casserole from the freezer to the refrigerator the day before cooking to fully thaw. Once it is fully thawed, follow all of the instructions for cook night to cook and serve.

NOTE: If you'd prefer to make the sauce from scratch, see page 227 for the Alfredo Sauce recipe.

GREEK SALMON SALAD WITH HERBY POTATO SALAD

Serves 4 on cook night and 4 on reheat night with the additional fresh ingredients found in the reheat grocery list on page 63

Greek salads are so wonderful because they are packed full of flavorful veggies. This one is especially fast and easy because the salmon cooks so quickly *and* we're using a clean, store-bought Greek dressing. Making your own Greek dressing (page 231) takes this salad up a notch if you have a few extra minutes—the fresh herbs bring the salad and the salmon to life. You'll be surprised how filling this is, especially with the potato salad.

SALMON

1 tsp olive oil

4 (6-oz [170-g]) salmon fillets

½ (8-oz [236-ml]) jar Paleo-friendly Greek dressing

2 heads romaine lettuce, chopped into 1-inch (2.5-cm) slices

1 pint (510 g) cherry tomatoes, sliced in half

1 cucumber, roughly chopped

½ red onion, ½-inch (1.3-cm) dice

¼ cup (45 g) Kalamata olives, pitted

1 banana pepper, thinly sliced

1 (6-oz [170-g]) Paleo feta block, crumbled

POTATO SALAD

Cooked red potatoes from the weekly prep (page 50)

½ (8-oz [236-ml]) jar Paleo-friendly Greek dressing

1 tsp salt

2 scallions, chopped

PREP DAY:

See page 50 for the prep ingredients and instructions.

COOK NIGHT:

Preheat the oven to 400°F (204°C).

Grease a shallow glass baking dish with the olive oil. Place the salmon skin-side down and pour ½ cup (120 ml) of the dressing on top. Cook the salmon for 10 to 15 minutes, or until the edges have started to flake.

Remove the cooked potatoes from the refrigerator, toss them with ½ cup (120 ml) of Greek dressing, season them with the salt, garnish with chopped scallions, then set aside.

To serve your salad, plate a bed of lettuce, top with the cherry tomatoes, cucumber, red onion, Kalamata olives, banana pepper and feta, and finish with the salmon fillets and a side of potato salad.

REHEAT NIGHT:

Chop and boil the potatoes using the instructions from prep day, then chill them in the refrigerator. Follow all of the cooking and serving instructions from cook night.

> **NOTE:** If you'd prefer to make the dressing from scratch, see page 231 for the Greek Dressing recipe.

MEDITERRANEAN QUICHE

Serves 4 on cook night and 4 on reheat night

I took a traditional quiche and packed it with delicious Mediterranean flavors. Sun-dried tomatoes are one of my secret ingredients—they really elevate the flavor of just about anything. Making your own crust will be absolutely worth the effort when you taste it!

1 quiche from the weekly prep (page 48)

PREP DAY:

See page 48 for the prep ingredients and instructions.

COOK NIGHT:

Preheat the oven to 350°F (177°C).

Remove the quiche from the refrigerator 30 minutes before warming. Remove the plastic wrap and aluminum foil. Save the foil for the next step.

Once the quiche is room temperature, wrap the foil around the crust or use a silicone crust cover.

Place the quiche in the oven and cook for 15 minutes, or until warmed through, being careful not to overcook. Cool slightly, slice into fourths and serve.

REHEAT NIGHT:

Move the quiche from the freezer to the refrigerator the day before serving. Then follow the cook night instructions.

WEEK 3 GROCERY LIST

PROTEIN

- [ ] 4 lbs (1.8 kg) turkey breast ● ●
- [ ] 2 lbs (907 g) or 8 (6-oz [170-g]) salmon fillets ● ●
- [ ] 18 eggs ●

PRODUCE

- [ ] 1 yellow onion ● ●
- [ ] 1 head garlic ● ● ●
- [ ] 2 stalks celery ● ●
- [ ] 1 red onion ● ●
- [ ] 4 heads romaine lettuce ● ●
- [ ] 1 bunch parsley, for garnish (optional) ●
- [ ] 3 lbs (1.4 kg) russet potatoes ●
- [ ] 1 (8-oz [226-g]) container baby bella mushrooms ●
- [ ] 1 green bell pepper ●
- [ ] 1 red bell pepper ●
- [ ] 1 bunch thyme ●
- [ ] 1 pint (510 g) cherry tomatoes ●
- [ ] 1 cucumber ●
- [ ] 4 shallots ●
- [ ] 8 cups (1 [5-oz (141-g)] package) baby spinach ●
- [ ] 1 bunch basil ●
- [ ] 2 lbs (907 g) red potatoes ●
- [ ] 1 bunch scallions ●
- [ ] 1 banana pepper ●

SPICES

- [ ] Herbs de Provence ● ●
- [ ] Smoked paprika ●
- [ ] Dried oregano ●
- [ ] Red pepper flakes ●

PANTRY

- [ ] 1 (32-oz [960-ml]) box chicken bone broth ● ●
- [ ] ¾ cup (177 ml) Paleo-friendly mayonnaise ●
- [ ] Maple syrup ●
- [ ] ½ cup (61 g) dried cranberries ●

- [ ] ½ cup (55 g) pecans ●
- [ ] ½ cup (27 g) sun-dried tomatoes ●
- [ ] ¼ cup (45 g) Kalamata olives ●
- [ ] 1 (4-oz [113-g]) jar pimientos ●
- [ ] Cassava flour ●
- [ ] Almond flour ●
- [ ] Coconut flour ●
- [ ] Tapioca starch ●
- [ ] Xanthan gum ●
- [ ] 2 cups (440 g) marinated artichoke hearts ●
- [ ] 2 (15.5-oz [440-g]) jars Paleo-friendly Alfredo sauce (I like Primal Kitchen No-Dairy Garlic Alfredo Sauce) ●
- [ ] 1 (8-oz [236-ml]) jar Paleo-friendly Greek dressing (I like Primal Kitchen Greek Vinaigrette & Marinade) ●
- [ ] 1 (12-oz [340-g]) jar Paleo-friendly romesco sauce (I like Chosen Foods Spanish Romesco Simmer Sauce) ●
- [ ] 1 cup (56 g) Paleo bread crumbs (I like Jeff Nathan Creations Chef Gourmet Panko Plain Gluten Free) ●

DAIRY ALTERNATIVES

- [ ] 1 cup plus 2 tbsp (237 g) unsalted ghee (I like Fourth & Heart) ● ●
- [ ] 1½ cups (355 ml) almond milk ●
- [ ] 1 (6-oz [170-g]) package Paleo-friendly feta (I like VioLife vegan feta) ●

FREEZER

- [ ] 1 cup (134 g) frozen peas ●
- [ ] 2 (9-oz [255-g]) frozen packages Paleo-friendly fettuccine-style noodles (I like Cappello's Fettuccine Noodles) ●

RECIPES KEY: ● ● ● ● ●

Southern Cranberry-Pecan Turkey Salad (page 52)
Sheet Pan Romesco Salmon with Patatas Bravas (page 55)
Not-Your-Mom's Turkey Tetrazzini (page 56)
Mediterranean Quiche (page 60)
Greek Salmon Salad with Herby Potato Salad (page 59)

WEEK 3 REHEAT GROCERY LIST

SOUTHERN CRANBERRY-PECAN TURKEY SALAD

- ☐ ¾ cup (177 ml) Paleo-friendly mayonnaise
- ☐ Maple syrup
- ☐ ½ cup (61 g) dried cranberries
- ☐ ½ cup (55 g) pecans
- ☐ 1 rib celery
- ☐ 1 red onion
- ☐ 2 heads romaine lettuce

SHEET PAN ROMESCO SALMON WITH PATATAS BRAVAS

- ☐ 3 lbs (1.4 kg) russet potatoes
- ☐ Paprika
- ☐ 1 lb (454 g) or 4 (6-oz [170-g]) salmon fillets
- ☐ 1 (12-oz [340-g]) jar Paleo-friendly romesco sauce (I like Chosen Foods Spanish Romesco Simmer Sauce)

NOT-YOUR-MOM'S TURKEY TETRAZZINI

- ☐ 1 bunch parsley, for garnish (optional)

GREEK SALMON SALAD WITH HERBY POTATO SALAD

- ☐ 1 lb (454 g) or 4 (6-oz [170-g]) salmon fillets
- ☐ 2 heads romaine lettuce
- ☐ 1 pint (510 g) cherry tomatoes
- ☐ 1 cucumber
- ☐ 1 red onion
- ☐ ¼ cup (45 g) Kalamata olives
- ☐ 1 banana pepper
- ☐ 2 lbs (907 g) red potatoes
- ☐ 1 bunch scallions
- ☐ 1 (6-oz [170-g]) package Paleo-friendly feta (I like VioLife vegan feta)
- ☐ 1 (8-oz [236-ml]) jar Paleo-friendly Greek dressing (I like Primal Kitchen Greek Vinaigrette & Marinade)

MEDITERRANEAN QUICHE

- ☐ Nothing needed

WEEK 4

Week 4 features chicken breast and pork shoulder, which are two of my favorite proteins! There is such a wide array of flavors this week: Mexican, Asian, Italian and Indian.

Beans are one of my very favorite foods. Unfortunately, not only are they not Paleo, but I found out recently I'm also severely intolerant to most types. Enter my "refried beans" recipe! They are packed with flavor and taste so much like the real thing. You'll want to make them with every Mexican meal. The mashed potatoes are such a classic side that you can pair with just about anything. And the breading for the crispy honey chicken I use for any Asian dish and switch out the sauces. I keep the breaded chicken piccata breasts in the freezer and my kiddos will eat them any time—you can even slice them like chicken fingers!

WEEK 4 PREP-DAY INSTRUCTIONS

This prep day starts off super easy with an Instant Pot recipe that cooks the pork all at once for the Paleo Pork Pozole Verde and Tacos al Pastor. No Instant Pot? No worries! It can also be made on your stovetop and in your oven. I absolutely love this Creamy Chicken Piccata over Mashed Potatoes recipe because it's deceptively simple and yet so gourmet! The Yellow Thai Pumpkin Curry is such a flavorful vegetarian dish. The crispy honey chicken sauce and kung pao sauces are some of my favorites in the whole book. Enjoy your prep day!

Step 1:

PALEO PORK POZOLE VERDE & PORK TACOS AL PASTOR WITH "REFRIED BEANS"

2 tbsp (30 ml) olive oil

4 lbs (1.8 kg) pork shoulder

Salt and pepper

1 (15-oz [425-g]) jar Paleo-friendly green chile sauce

6 cups (1.4 L) chicken bone broth

Make the pulled pork for the pozole and the tacos recipes in your Instant Pot (if you don't have an Instant Pot, skip to the next paragraph). Start by setting the Instant Pot to sauté and add the olive oil. Season the pork with salt and pepper. Add the pork to the Instant Pot and sear on all sides (you can cut the pork into chunks if necessary to fit it into the Instant Pot). Turn off the sauté setting and pour in the green chile sauce and bone broth. Cover and set the Instant Pot to Stew for 1 hour.

If you do not have an Instant Pot, preheat the oven to 300°F (149°C). Heat the olive oil in a large Dutch oven over medium-high heat. Season the pork with salt and pepper and sear it in the Dutch oven until it's browned on all sides, 3 to 4 minutes per side. Feel free to divide the pork in half or thirds to make it easier to sauté. Once the pork is seared, remove it from the pot and add ½ cup (120 ml) of bone broth to the pot and scrape off all the brown bits. Return the pork to the pot, then add the green chile sauce and remaining bone broth. Cover the pot and place it in the oven to cook for 2 to 3 hours. Check the internal temperature of the pork using a meat thermometer. When it reaches 180 to 190°F (82 to 88°C), remove it from the oven (this is a higher temperature than normal, but the higher temperature is necessary to break down the collagen and give you that pull-apart tenderness).

Step 2:

CREAMY CHICKEN PICCATA OVER MASHED POTATOES

2½ lbs (1.1 kg) boneless, skinless chicken breasts

1 cup (95 g) almond meal

⅓ cup (43 g) tapioca starch

1 tbsp (5 g) nutritional yeast

2 tsp (12 g) salt

1 tsp black pepper

4 tbsp (60 g) ghee, divided

4 tbsp (60 ml) olive oil, divided

While the pork is cooking, slice the chicken breasts in half crosswise to create cutlets. Place each cutlet on a cutting board and lightly pound until thin (about ½ inch [1.3 cm] thick).

In a shallow dish, whisk together the almond meal, tapioca starch, nutritional yeast, salt and pepper.

In a large nonstick skillet, heat 2 tablespoons (30 g) of ghee with 2 tablespoons (30 ml) of olive oil. Dredge each chicken breast through the flour mixture and, working in batches, cook the cutlets in the pan for about 2 minutes on each side, until golden brown and cooked through. Transfer the chicken cutlets to a plate. Add the remaining 2 tablespoons (30 g) of ghee and 2 tablespoons (30 ml) of olive oil as needed to cook all the cutlets.

Set the cutlets aside to cool. Once the cutlets have cooled, divide them into two equal portions. Carefully wrap each portion in parchment or wax paper and lay flat in a reseal-able or stasher bag. Store one portion in the refrigerator for cook night and the other portion in the freezer for reheat night.

Step 3:

YELLOW THAI PUMPKIN CURRY

1 (16-oz [454-g]) jar Paleo-friendly yellow curry sauce

1 (15-oz [425-g]) can pumpkin puree

1 (13.5-oz [398-ml]) can coconut milk

3 shallots, cut in half

2 small butternut squashes, peeled and diced, or 2 (15-oz [425-g]) containers

2 sweet potatoes, diced

4 carrots, sliced

2 crowns broccoli, chopped into bite-sized pieces

Zest and juice of 1 lime

Salt and pepper, to taste

After storing the chicken piccata, move on to the pumpkin curry. In a large pot, pour in the yellow curry sauce, pumpkin puree and coconut milk and stir until combined. Bring to a simmer over medium heat and let simmer uncovered for 5 minutes.

Add the shallots, butternut squashes, sweet potatoes, carrots and broccoli to the pot and simmer, uncovered, until the vegetables are tender, 10 to 15 minutes.

Add the zest and juice from the lime and stir to combine.

Season to taste with salt and pepper.

Allow the curry to completely cool and divide it into two even portions. Place each portion in an airtight container. Store one portion in the refrigerator for cook night and the other portion in the freezer for reheat night.

Step 4:

PORK TACOS AL PASTOR WITH "REFRIED BEANS"

4 cups (438 g) raw cashews, divided

3 tbsp (15 g) Paleo-friendly taco seasoning blend

¾ cup (180 ml) beef bone broth, plus more to thin if needed

After storing the pumpkin curry, make the "refried beans." Place 2 cups (219 g) of cashews in a bowl and cover them with boiling water. Let sit for 15 minutes to soften, then drain the water.

While those cashews are softening, add the remaining 2 cups (219 g) of cashews and the taco seasoning blend into a food processor and process. Once the mixture turns into a powder, start adding the beef bone broth slowly. Add additional broth if needed to reach the desired consistency. Once the mixture is completely blended, add to a mixing bowl.

Add the softened cashews to the mixing bowl and stir to combine.

Divide the "refried beans" into two even portions and place each portion in an airtight container. Store one portion in the refrigerator for cook night and the other portion in the freezer for reheat night.

CRISPY HONEY CHICKEN WITH KUNG PAO BRUSSELS

HONEY SAUCE

2 tbsp (30 ml) sesame oil

6 cloves garlic, minced

1 (2-inch [5-cm]) piece ginger, finely grated on a microplane

6 tbsp (90 ml) coconut aminos

2 tbsp (30 ml) rice vinegar

2 cups (480 ml) honey

After storing the "refried beans," make the honey sauce for the chicken. In a small saucepan on the stovetop, heat the sesame oil over medium heat. Add the garlic and ginger and sauté until fragrant, about 2 minutes. Add the coconut aminos, rice vinegar and honey and bring to a gentle simmer. Simmer uncovered for 5 minutes, then remove from the heat and cool.

KUNG PAO SAUCE

1 cup (240 ml) sesame oil, divided

8 cloves garlic, minced

¼ cup (60 ml) white wine vinegar

1 cup (240 ml) coconut aminos

4 tsp (10 g) arrowroot

1 cup (240 g) chile-garlic paste

½ tsp Sichuan peppers (optional)

1 cup (200 g) coconut sugar

While the honey sauce is cooking and cooling, make the kung pao sauce for the Brussels. In another small saucepan on the stovetop, heat ¼ cup (60 ml) of sesame oil over medium heat. Add the garlic and sauté until fragrant, about 2 minutes. Add the remaining ingredients (including the remaining ¾ cup [180 ml] sesame oil) and whisk to combine. Bring to a boil, then reduce the heat to a simmer and simmer the sauce uncovered until thickened, 10 to 15 minutes. Remove from the heat and cool.

1½ lbs (680 g) Brussels sprouts

While the kung pao sauce is cooking, prepare the Brussels sprouts by trimming the ends and slicing them in half lengthwise. Store in an airtight container in the refrigerator for cook night.

4 lbs (1.8 kg) boneless, skinless chicken breasts

Prepare the chicken by cutting each breast into 1-inch (2.5-cm) cubes. Divide the amount of cubed chicken in half. Store one portion in an airtight container in the refrigerator for cook night and the other portion in an airtight container in the freezer for reheat night.

When both sauces have cooled, divide each sauce into two equal portions. Store one portion in the refrigerator for cook night and the other portion in the freezer for reheat night.

CREAMY CHICKEN PICCATA OVER MASHED POTATOES

2½ lbs (1.1 kg) russet potatoes

1½ tbsp (27 g) kosher salt

1 (13.5-oz [398-ml]) can coconut milk

2 cloves garlic, minced

2 tbsp (30 g) unsalted ghee

½ tsp black pepper

After prepping the crispy honey chicken, make the mashed potatoes by chopping the potatoes into even-sized pieces and adding them to a large pot. Cover the potatoes with cold water and add the salt. Bring the water to a boil and cook the potatoes for 10 to 15 minutes until the potatoes are fork-tender. Drain the potatoes, then return them to the pot and add the coconut milk, garlic, ghee and pepper. Use a potato masher and mash the ingredients together until you reach the desired consistency, or feel free to add all the ingredients to a mixer with the paddle attachment and mix until well blended. Allow to cool, then place in an airtight container for cook night.

PALEO PORK POZOLE VERDE

1 bunch cilantro

2 cups (292 g) raw cashews

2 cups (480 ml) chicken bone broth

Juice of 1 lime

Salt and pepper, to taste

After you have made and stored the mashed potatoes, and once the Instant Pot timer (if using) is up for the pork, manually release the steam vent from the Instant Pot. Carefully remove the pork from the Instant Pot (or Dutch oven if you made it without the Instant Pot) and place it on a large cutting board. Once the pork is cool enough to handle, shred it using two forks.

Divide the shredded pork into two portions (one portion for the Paleo Pork Pozole Verde and the other portion for the Pork Tacos al Pastor). Divide the pork for the Pork Tacos al Pastor into two airtight containers. Store one in the refrigerator for cook night and the other in the freezer for reheat night.

Add the remaining contents from the Instant Pot or Dutch Oven to a blender. Add the cilantro (both leaves and stems) and blend until smooth. Return the sauce to the Instant Pot and set to Keep Warm.

Return the portion of shredded pork for the pozole back to the Instant Pot with the cashews and chicken bone broth and stir to combine. Add the juice from the lime and season to taste with salt and pepper.

Turn the Instant Pot off and allow the pozole to completely cool. Divide it into two even portions and place each portion in an airtight container. Store one portion in the refrigerator for cook night and the other portion in the freezer for reheat week.

YELLOW THAI PUMPKIN CURRY

Serves 4 on cook night and 4 on reheat night with the additional fresh ingredients found in the reheat grocery list on page 81

Sometimes I need a break from heavier meat-based dishes, so I love to incorporate a vegetarian meal into my weekly rotation. This pumpkin curry is such a fun rendition of a vegetable yellow curry. It's the perfect fall meal, but you can really mix it up with any of your favorite vegetables to make it a year-long staple. I use this recipe as a general guideline, then switch up the type of vegetables and curries to make completely new variations.

½ recipe yellow Thai pumpkin curry from the weekly prep (page 67)

½ cup (8 g) cilantro, for garnish (optional)

3 tbsp (22 g) toasted pumpkin seeds, for garnish (optional)

PREP DAY:

See page 67 for the prep ingredients and instructions.

COOK NIGHT:

Remove the curry from the refrigerator and reheat on the stovetop in a large pot over medium-high heat.

Once heated through, serve hot and top with optional garnishes such as chopped cilantro and toasted pumpkin seeds.

REHEAT NIGHT:

To thaw the curry overnight, move it from the freezer to the refrigerator the night before reheat night. To thaw day of, move the container from the freezer to your countertop and allow the curry to completely thaw at room temperature. For a quick thaw, submerge the container in room temperature water until completely thawed. Once thawed, follow all of the instructions from cook night.

> **NOTE:** If you'd prefer to make the curry sauce from scratch, see page 231 for the Pumpkin Yellow Curry Sauce recipe.

PORK TACOS AL PASTOR WITH "REFRIED BEANS"

Serves 4 on cook night and 4 on reheat night with the additional fresh ingredients found in the reheat grocery list on page 81

I could eat tacos for every single meal, and tacos al pastor are some of my very favorite. There is such a mix of flavors in this version because it was inspired by the lamb shawarma that was brought to Mexico by Lebanese immigrants. To make this dish less spicy and more kid-friendly, add the guajillo and arbol chiles a little bit at a time until you reach your desired level of heat.

PINEAPPLE SALSA

2 cups (330 g) fresh pineapple, ¼-inch (6-mm) dice

¼ cup (40 g) red onion, ¼-inch (6-mm) dice

⅓ cup (5 g) cilantro, roughly chopped

Juice from 1 lime

½ jalapeño, seeded and finely chopped (optional)

½ tsp salt

PORK

1 (12-oz [340-g]) jar Paleo-friendly pastor sauce

2 lbs (907 g) shredded pork with green chiles from the weekly prep (page 66)

CASHEW "REFRIED BEANS"

½ portion cashew "refried beans" from the weekly prep (page 67)

FOR SERVING

1 (8-piece) package taco-sized grain-free tortillas

PREP DAY:

See page 66 for the prep ingredients and instructions.

COOK NIGHT:

Make the pineapple salsa by combining all the ingredients in a bowl and mixing together. Set aside.

Remove the pastor sauce, shredded pork and "refried beans" from the refrigerator.

Combine the pastor sauce and the shredded pork and add to a pan on the stovetop over medium heat. Heat until warmed through.

Add the "refried beans" to a separate pot on the stovetop over medium heat. Heat until warmed through (you may add a little broth if the beans are too thick).

Warm your tortillas according to the package directions.

Build your tacos and serve with the pineapple salsa and "refried beans."

REHEAT NIGHT:

To thaw the shredded pork and "refried beans" overnight, move them from the freezer to the refrigerator the night before reheat night. To thaw day of, move each container from the freezer to your countertop and allow the sauce, pork and "beans" to completely thaw at room temperature. For a quick thaw, submerge each container in room temperature water until completely thawed. Once thawed, follow the instructions for cook night.

NOTE: If you'd prefer to make your seasoning blend and pastor sauce from scratch, see page 231 for the Taco Seasoning recipe and page 232 for the Tacos al Pastor Sauce recipe.

CRISPY HONEY CHICKEN WITH KUNG PAO BRUSSELS

Serves 4 on cook night and 4 on reheat night with the additional fresh ingredients found in the reheat grocery list on page 81

This meal is a great takeout replacement! I use this same breading and frying technique for any Asian dish, and then just swap out the sauce and the veggies. These crispy honey chicken nuggets are a huge crowd-pleaser for adults and kiddos alike!

½ portion honey sauce from the weekly prep (page 68)

½ portion kung pao sauce from the weekly prep (page 68)

Olive oil, for frying

⅔ cup (85 g) tapioca starch

2 tsp (12 g) salt

½ portion cubed chicken breasts from the weekly prep (page 68)

1 portion Brussels sprouts from the weekly prep (page 68)

⅓ cup (16 g) scallions, thinly sliced

¼ cup (27 g) sliced almonds, pine nuts or cashews (optional)

PREP DAY:

See page 68 for the prep ingredients and instructions.

COOK NIGHT:

Remove the honey and the kung pao sauces from the refrigerator.

In a large skillet with high sides, heat ½ inch (1.3 cm) of olive oil over medium-high heat. Mix the tapioca starch and salt in a shallow dish, then toss the chicken in the mixture until it's well coated.

Working in batches, carefully add the cubed chicken to the hot oil and fry until golden brown and cooked through (165°F [74°C]). Line a plate with paper towels. Using tongs, remove the chicken from the oil and place it onto the prepared plate to absorb any oil.

While the chicken cooks, in a large skillet, heat 2 tablespoons (30 ml) of olive oil over medium heat and place the Brussels sprouts in the skillet cut side down. Fry for 5 to 7 minutes without moving them, until they're slightly brown on the flat side and bright green on the outside.

While the chicken and Brussels sprouts are cooking, reheat the honey and kung pao sauces in individual saucepans on the stovetop or in individual heatproof bowls in the microwave.

Put the cooked chicken in a bowl, pour the warmed honey sauce over it and toss to coat. Garnish with the sliced scallions and almonds (if using). Once the Brussels sprouts are done, toss them in the kung pao sauce and top them with the scallions and almonds. Toss to coat. Serve the crispy honey chicken with a side of the Brussels sprouts.

REHEAT NIGHT:

To thaw the chicken and honey and kung pao sauces overnight, move them from the freezer to the refrigerator the night before reheat night. To thaw day of, move them from the freezer to your countertop to completely thaw at room temperature. For a quick thaw, submerge each container in room temperature water until completely thawed. Measure out the tapioca starch and salt and set aside. Follow the instructions for cook night.

PALEO PORK POZOLE VERDE

Serves 4 on cook night and 4 on reheat night with the additional fresh ingredients found in the reheat grocery list on page 81

This Paleo Pork Pozole Verde combines my love for Mexican food and my love for soups. Typically, it's made with hominy, which is corn kernels treated with lye or lime. Instead, I use cooked cashews, which give us a similar taste and texture. The tomatillos and peppers give this pozole its unique smoky flavors.

½ recipe Paleo pork pozole verde made from the weekly prep (page 66)

Avocado, for garnish (optional)

Lime wedges, for garnish (optional)

Radishes, sliced, for garnish (optional)

Cilantro, for garnish (optional)

PREP DAY:

See page 66 for the prep ingredients and instructions.

COOK NIGHT:

Remove the pozole from the refrigerator and put it in a pot on the stovetop. Reheat over medium heat until warmed through.

Serve in bowls and top with avocado, lime wedges, radishes and cilantro, if using.

REHEAT NIGHT:

Move the pozole from the freezer to the refrigerator the night before or from the freezer to the countertop the morning of to thaw. Put the thawed pozole in a pot on the stovetop. Reheat over medium heat.

Serve in bowls and top with avocado, lime wedges, radishes and cilantro, if using.

NOTE: If you'd prefer to make your own Green Chile Sauce from scratch, see page 229 for the recipe.

CREAMY CHICKEN PICCATA OVER MASHED POTATOES

Serves 4 on cook night and 4 on reheat night with the additional fresh ingredients found in the reheat grocery list on page 81

You will be shocked at how much flavor this dish packs given how easy it is to make! I typically make a lot of these breaded chicken breasts and freeze them so I have them on hand for a 10-minute meal. This piccata sauce is made with lemon juice, ghee, broth and capers. The coconut cream and arrowroot transform it into a creamy piccata sauce. Served over mashed potatoes, this is a delectable comfort meal.

1 recipe mashed potatoes from the weekly prep (page 69)

½ recipe chicken piccata from the weekly prep (page 66)

4 tbsp (60 g) unsalted ghee, divided

2 cloves garlic, minced

1 small shallot, finely chopped

½ cup (120 ml) chicken bone broth, plus more if needed

⅓ cup (80 ml) lemon juice

¼ cup (45 g) capers, drained

1 tsp salt

1 (5-oz [141-g]) can coconut cream

2 tsp (5 g) arrowroot

Parsley, chopped, for garnish

PREP DAY:

See page 66 for the prep ingredients and instructions.

COOK NIGHT:

Remove the mashed potatoes from the refrigerator and put them in a pot on the stovetop. Reheat over medium heat, stirring occasionally, until warmed through. You may add a bit of chicken broth if necessary.

Remove the chicken cutlets from the refrigerator, unwrap them, place them on a large plate and set aside. While the potatoes are reheating, melt 2 tablespoons (30 g) of the ghee in a large straight-sided sauté pan over medium heat. Add the minced garlic and shallot and sauté until the shallot is tender and fragrant, 1 to 2 minutes. Deglaze the pan with the chicken broth and scrape off the browned bits from the bottom of the pan. Add the lemon juice, capers and salt.

Add the chicken cutlets to the pan and simmer, uncovered, until the chicken is warmed through and the sauce has thickened a bit, 5 to 7 minutes, turning the cutlets halfway through.

In a small bowl, combine the coconut cream and arrowroot. Whisk, then slowly add the mixture to the piccata in the pan. Stir to combine and heat through.

To serve, spoon the mashed potatoes into a large circle in the middle of each plate, add the chicken picatta with sauce and garnish with chopped parsley.

REHEAT NIGHT:

To thaw the breaded chicken, move it from the freezer to the refrigerator the night before reheat night. Make the mashed potatoes using the instructions on prep day, then follow the instructions for cook night.

WEEK 4 GROCERY LIST

PROTEIN
- ☐ 6½ lbs (2.7 kg) boneless, skinless chicken breast ● ●
- ☐ 4 lbs (1.8 kg) pork shoulder ● ●

PRODUCE
- ☐ 4 shallots ● ●
- ☐ 1 (2-inch [5-cm]) piece fresh ginger ●
- ☐ 2 heads garlic ● ●
- ☐ 2 small butternut squashes (or 2 [15-oz (425-g)] bags frozen) ●
- ☐ 2 sweet potatoes ●
- ☐ 4 carrots ●
- ☐ 2 broccoli crowns ●
- ☐ 4 limes ● ● ●
- ☐ 2 bunches cilantro ● ● ●
- ☐ 2 cups (330 g) diced pineapple ●
- ☐ 1 red onion ●
- ☐ 1 jalapeño ●
- ☐ 1½ lbs (680 g) Brussels sprouts ●
- ☐ 1 bunch scallions ●
- ☐ 2 avocados ●
- ☐ 1 small bunch radishes ●
- ☐ ⅓ cup (79 ml) lemon juice ●
- ☐ 1 bunch flat-leaf parsley ●
- ☐ 2½ lbs (1.1 kg) russet potatoes ●

SPICES
- ☐ 3 tbsp (15 g) taco seasoning (I like Siete Taco Seasoning) ●

PANTRY
- ☐ 1 (15-oz [425-g]) can pumpkin puree ●
- ☐ 2 (13.5-oz [398-ml]) cans coconut milk ● ●
- ☐ 6 cups (876 g) raw cashews ● ●
- ☐ 1 (32-oz [960-ml]) box beef bone broth ●
- ☐ Tapioca starch ● ●
- ☐ Sesame oil ●
- ☐ 1⅓ cups (320 ml) coconut aminos ●
- ☐ Rice vinegar ●
- ☐ 2 cups (480 ml) honey ●

- ☐ ¼ cup (59 ml) white wine vinegar ●
- ☐ Arrowroot ●
- ☐ Chile-garlic paste ●
- ☐ ½ tsp Sichuan peppers (optional) ●
- ☐ Coconut sugar ●
- ☐ ¼ cup (59 ml) sliced almonds ●
- ☐ 3 (32-oz [960-ml]) boxes chicken bone broth ● ● ●
- ☐ Almond meal ●
- ☐ Nutritional yeast ●
- ☐ ¼ cup (45 g) capers ●
- ☐ 1 (5-oz [141-g]) can coconut cream ●
- ☐ 3 tbsp (22 g) pumpkin seeds (pepitas) ●
- ☐ 1 (12-oz [340-g]) jar Paleo-friendly pastor sauce (I like Chosen Foods Guajillo-Pasilla Chile Simmer Sauce) ●
- ☐ 1 (15-oz [425-g]) jar Paleo-friendly green chile sauce (I like Siete Green Enchilada Sauce) ● ●
- ☐ 1 (16-oz [454-g]) jar Paleo-friendly yellow curry sauce (I like Yai's Thai Yellow Thai Coconut Curry) ●

DAIRY ALTERNATIVES
- ☐ 8 tbsp (118 g) unsalted ghee (I like Fourth & Heart) ●

FREEZER
- ☐ 1 (8-piece) package taco-sized grain-free tortillas (I like Siete Cassava Tortillas) ●

RECIPES KEY: ● ● ● ● ●

Pork Tacos al Pastor with "Refried Beans" (page 73)
Crispy Honey Chicken with Kung Pao Brussels (page 74)
Paleo Pork Pozole Verde (page 77)
Yellow Thai Pumpkin Curry (page 70)
Creamy Chicken Piccata over Mashed Potatoes (page 78)

WEEK 4 REHEAT GROCERY LIST

YELLOW THAI PUMPKIN CURRY

☐ 1 bunch cilantro

☐ 3 tbsp (27 g) pumpkin seeds (pepitas)

PORK TACOS AL PASTOR WITH "REFRIED BEANS"

☐ 1 (12-oz [340-g]) jar Paleo-friendly pastor sauce (I like Chosen Foods Guajillo-Pasilla Chile Simmer Sauce)

☐ 2 cups (330 g) diced pineapple

☐ 1 red onion

☐ 1 bunch cilantro

☐ 1 lime

☐ 1 jalapeño

☐ 1 (8-piece) package taco-sized grain-free tortillas

CRISPY HONEY CHICKEN WITH KUNG PAO BRUSSELS

☐ 1 bunch scallions

☐ 1½ lbs (680 g) Brussels sprouts

☐ ¼ cup (27 g) sliced almonds

☐ Tapioca starch

PALEO PORK POZOLE VERDE

☐ 2 avocados

☐ 1 lime

☐ 1 small bunch radishes

☐ 1 bunch cilantro

CREAMY CHICKEN PICCATA OVER MASHED POTATOES

☐ 1 head garlic

☐ 1 shallot

☐ 1 (32-oz [960-ml]) box chicken bone broth

☐ ⅓ cup (80 ml) lemon juice

☐ ¼ cup (45 g) capers

☐ 1 (5-oz [141-g]) can coconut cream

☐ Arrowroot

☐ 1 bunch flat-leaf parsley

☐ 2½ lbs (1.1 kg) russet potatoes

☐ 1 (13.5-oz [398-ml]) can coconut milk

☐ Unsalted ghee (I like Fourth & Heart)

WEEK 5

This week feels extremely homey to me and includes some of my favorite childhood foods. Lasagna is such a staple in so many homes, so I'm thrilled to be able to enjoy those cozy flavors without the gluten and dairy! Almost every Sunday after church growing up, we ate at the same restaurant and the hush puppies were my favorite part. I created my mini hush puppy muffins as a tribute to those memories. We make this Five-Pepper Sweet Potato Chili (a blog favorite!) so much that I like to think it will be one of the recipes my kiddos fondly remember one day. If the flavors this week are new to you, I hope you embrace them and love them as much as I do.

WEEK 5 PREP-DAY INSTRUCTIONS

I absolutely love keeping an extra homestyle lasagna in the freezer to pull out whenever we need a quick, hearty meal, and you'll be able to do the same after this week's prep day! The Make-Ahead Homestyle Lasagna and the Five-Pepper Sweet Potato Chili make a great cooking duo because you start both recipes at the same time and let them simmer away on the stove while you move on to the next steps. The battered cod is so worth the effort—and the hush puppy muffins are the perfect counterpart. I love how fast the buffalo cauliflower tacos come together. I just know you'll love these cod cakes so much you'll always keep some in the freezer for a quick-and-easy meal!

Step 1:

MAKE-AHEAD HOMESTYLE LASAGNA

2 (9-oz [255-g]) packages Cappello's Lasagna Sheets

Preheat the oven to 350°F (177°C), then remove the lasagna noodles from the freezer and allow them to thaw.

Step 2:

FIVE-PEPPER SWEET POTATO CHILI & MAKE-AHEAD HOMESTYLE LASAGNA

CHILI

2 tbsp (30 ml) olive oil

1 yellow onion, diced

2 lbs (907 g) ground beef

4 cloves garlic, minced (or ½ tsp garlic powder)

MAKE-AHEAD HOMESTYLE LASAGNA

2 tbsp (30 ml) olive oil

1 yellow onion, cut into ½-inch (1.3-cm) dice

2 lbs (907 g) ground beef

4 cloves garlic, minced (or ½ tsp garlic powder)

While your lasagna noodles are thawing, you will brown the ground beef for both of these recipes simultaneously. Use two large soup pots or Dutch ovens.

In both pots, heat the olive oil over medium heat. Add the onion and beef and cook until the onion is translucent and the beef is browned, about 10 minutes. Add the garlic and cook until fragrant, about 1 more minute.

Step 3:

MAKE-AHEAD HOMESTYLE LASAGNA

1 tsp red pepper flakes (optional)

8 cups (1.9 L) Paleo-friendly marinara sauce

After the ground beef mixture is fully cooked, add the red pepper flakes, if using, and the marinara sauce to only one pot of the ground beef mixture and simmer, uncovered, for 20 minutes.

Step 4:

FIVE-PEPPER SWEET POTATO CHILI

2 tbsp (15 g) chili powder

1 tbsp (5 g) cumin

½ tsp paprika

1 tsp dried oregano

1 tbsp (18 g) salt

1 (28-oz [794-g]) can diced tomatoes

1 red bell pepper, chopped

1 green bell pepper, chopped

1 yellow bell pepper, chopped

1 jalapeño, chopped

1 poblano pepper, chopped

3 cups (402 g) sweet potatoes, peeled and chopped

To the pot for the chili, add the chili powder, cumin, paprika, oregano, salt, diced tomatoes, bell peppers, jalapeño, poblano pepper and the sweet potatoes.

Bring the chili to a boil, then simmer, covered, for 30 minutes.

Step 5:

MAKE-AHEAD HOMESTYLE LASAGNA

1 (32-oz [907-g]) container Kite Hill nondairy ricotta

2 tsp (2 g) dried oregano

3 eggs, gently whisked

2 tsp (6 g) salt

1 tsp black pepper

1 cup (24 g) fresh basil leaves, torn

While the lasagna sauce and chili are cooking, in a bowl, combine the ricotta, dried oregano, eggs, salt and black pepper. Stir to combine.

Remove the lasagna sauce from the heat and stir in the basil.

Spray two 8 x 8–inch (20 x 20–cm) baking dishes with avocado oil cooking spray.

Spread ½ cup (120 ml) of the lasagna sauce along the bottom of each baking dish. Arrange one layer of thawed noodles in each dish, followed by a layer of meat sauce and then a few large dollops of the ricotta mixture. Repeat this layering pattern twice more, finishing both lasagnas with a top layer of ricotta.

In your preheated oven, bake both lasagnas for 40 minutes.

Step 6:

FIVE-PEPPER SWEET POTATO CHILI

Once the chili is done, allow it to cool. Store half in an airtight container in the refrigerator and half in an airtight container in the freezer.

Step 7:

CRISPY BATTERED COD, SLAW AND HUSH PUPPY MUFFINS

BATTER

1 cup (125 g) tapioca starch

¼ cup (31 g) cassava flour

½ tsp paprika

½ tsp garlic salt

½ tsp salt

½ tsp black pepper

In a medium, shallow rectangular storage container with a lid, mix together the tapioca starch, cassava flour, paprika, garlic salt, salt and pepper. Close the top and keep this mixture at room temperature until cook night.

(continued)

HUSH PUPPY MINI MUFFINS

1 cup (125 g) cassava flour

1 cup (95 g) almond flour

½ tsp baking soda

2 tbsp (16 g) monk fruit extract

¾ tsp garlic powder

¾ tsp onion powder

¾ tsp paprika

1 tsp salt

¼ tsp black pepper

½ yellow onion (about 1 cup [160 g]), ⅛-inch (3-mm) dice

1 egg

1 cup (240 ml) coconut milk

1 tbsp (15 ml) lemon juice

Next, prepare the dry ingredients to make the hush puppy muffins. In a large mixing bowl, mix together the cassava flour, almond flour, baking soda, monk fruit, garlic powder, onion powder, paprika, salt and pepper. Add the onion, and stir until the onion is coated.

In a separate small mixing bowl, whisk together the egg, coconut milk and lemon juice. Add the wet ingredients to the dry ingredients and stir until just combined.

Grease your muffin pan.

For a mini muffin pan, fill them to the top of the tin and bake in the preheated oven (with the lasagnas) for 10 to 15 minutes, until they are golden brown on top and a cake tester or toothpick comes out clean.

For a full-sized muffin pan, fill them to the top and bake in the preheated oven for 25 to 30 minutes, until they are golden brown on top and a cake tester or toothpick comes out clean.

Freeze half of the muffins in an airtight container and store the other half in an airtight container in the refrigerator.

Step 8:

MAKE-AHEAD HOMESTYLE LASAGNA

Once the lasagnas are done baking, remove them from the oven (keep the oven on at 350°F [177°C] for the hush puppies) and allow both lasagnas to completely cool. Cover both of the lasagnas with plastic wrap tightly, then also wrap them in aluminum foil. Put one in the refrigerator for cook night and one in the freezer for reheat night.

Step 9:

LEMONY COD CAKES OVER CAESAR SALAD

2 lbs (907 g) cod fillets, or other white flaky fish

2 bay leaves

2 lemons, sliced

2 tsp (12 g) salt

1 tsp black pepper

4 tbsp (60 ml) olive oil

2 shallots, diced

4 ribs celery, diced

4 cloves garlic, minced

After your lasagnas are cooled and stored, you'll move on to the lemony cod cakes. To poach the cod, put the cod in a large saucepan and cover with water. Add the bay leaves, lemon slices, salt and pepper. Bring to a simmer, cover and cook for 3 to 4 minutes, until the cod is cooked through and flaky.

While the cod is poaching, heat the olive oil in a skillet over medium-high heat, add the shallots and celery and sauté until translucent, 4 to 5 minutes. During this time, drain the water from the poached cod and set the cod aside to cool.

Add the garlic to the shallot-and-celery skillet and sauté until fragrant, about 1 minute more. Transfer to a bowl on the side to cool.

2 tbsp (30 ml) Paleo-friendly mayonnaise

4 tsp (20 ml) Dijon mustard

4 eggs

3 tsp (18 g) salt

1 tsp black pepper

2 tsp (2 g) paprika

½ tsp red pepper flakes

2 cups (112 g) Paleo-friendly bread crumbs

In a small bowl, combine the mayonnaise, mustard, eggs, salt, pepper, paprika, red pepper flakes and bread crumbs. Mix well and add this mixture to the bowl of cooked shallots and celery.

Flake the poached cod and carefully add it to the bowl, gently mixing to combine ingredients.

Form this mixture into eight cod cake patties and place onto a parchment paper–lined sheet pan. Place the sheet pan in the refrigerator to cool for 30 minutes to set.

Step 10:

CRUNCHY BUFFALO CAULIFLOWER TACOS WITH A WEDGE SALAD

1 head cauliflower, chopped into bite-sized florets

1 cup (117 g) walnuts, chopped

1 cup (240 ml) Paleo-friendly Buffalo sauce

While the cod cakes are setting in the refrigerator, you'll make the Buffalo cauliflower filling. Add the cauliflower florets and walnuts to a large storage container with the Buffalo sauce, and toss to coat. Store in the refrigerator for cook night.

Step 11:

LEMONY COD CAKES OVER CAESAR SALAD

Once your cod cake patties are set, transfer two sets of four patties to two separate storage containers with airtight lids, using parchment paper between layers for both sets. Store one container in the refrigerator if you'll be making the cod cakes within 3 days, or in the freezer if you'll be making them later. Store the other four patties in the freezer.

FIVE-PEPPER SWEET POTATO CHILI

Serves 4 on cook night and 4 on reheat night with the additional fresh ingredients found in the reheat grocery list on page 99

This recipe is a reader favorite on my blog; some readers tell me they make this chili weekly in the winters, and I do, too! The variety of peppers in this chili give it a great depth of flavor, and they are the perfect replacement for the typical beans in a traditional chili. Fun tip: If you love chocolate like I do, add a few squares of unsweetened baking chocolate at the end. You'll thank me later!

½ recipe five-pepper sweet potato chili from the weekly prep (page 84)

Avocado, sliced, for serving

Cilantro, chopped, for serving

Radishes, sliced, for serving

PREP DAY:

See page 84 for the instructions to prep this recipe.

COOK NIGHT:

Remove the chili from the refrigerator, put it in a large pot and warm it over low heat until it reaches your desired temperature, about 10 minutes.

While that's warming, prepare any toppings you would like: sliced avocado, chopped cilantro and sliced radishes.

Serve the chili in bowls with any or all of the suggested toppings.

REHEAT NIGHT:

Remove the chili from the freezer the day before you are planning on serving it, and allow it to thaw in the refrigerator. Once it is fully thawed, use the instructions from cook night to warm and serve the chili.

LEMONY COD CAKES OVER CAESAR SALAD

Serves 4 on cook night and 4 on reheat night with the additional fresh ingredients found in the reheat grocery list on page 99

These cod cakes are so unique and versatile: You can use them on a salad (as you do here), serve them between buns as a burger or pair them with almost any side! The store-bought Caesar dressing makes this salad easy to whip together. But let me tell you—at some point, you have to try my Caesar dressing on page 232. It's truly the best Caesar dressing I've ever had, and I'm a huge Caesar salad fan! This cod cake twist on a traditional Caesar salad is tasty, filling and unique!

4 cod cakes from the weekly prep (page 86)

½ cup (120 ml) light olive oil, for frying

2 heads romaine lettuce

1 (10-oz [296-ml]) jar Paleo-friendly Caesar dressing

PREP DAY:
See page 86 for the prep ingredients and instructions.

COOK NIGHT:
Remove the cod cakes from the refrigerator.

Heat the oil in a large skillet over high heat. Add the cod cakes and sauté until golden brown, 4 to 5 minutes per side. Remove from the pan and keep warm.

Meanwhile, chop the romaine into 1-inch (2.5-cm) pieces.

Serve the cod cakes over the romaine and top with the Caesar dressing.

REHEAT NIGHT:
Remove the patties from the freezer a few hours before you plan to cook them and allow them to thaw only partially.

Heat the oil in a large skillet over high heat. Add the cod cakes and sauté until golden brown, 6 to 8 minutes per side. Remove from the pan and keep warm.

Follow the remaining instructions from cook night to pull this meal together.

> **NOTE:** If you'd prefer to make the dressing from scratch, see page 232 for the Caesar Dressing recipe.

MAKE-AHEAD HOMESTYLE LASAGNA

Serves 4 on cook night and 4 on reheat night

This lasagna is one of the most universal comfort foods in the entire cookbook. Combining pasta and a casserole might just be one of the greatest food inventions of all time. This recipe uses two of the best Paleo products on the market: Cappello's lasagna sheets and Kite Hill nondairy ricotta. With these two products, this homestyle lasagna tastes *just* like the real thing! The best part? It requires *zero* day-of prep so you'll have dinner from the refrigerator to your table in an hour with no time in the kitchen! It's the perfect meal for a busy weeknight.

1 precooked lasagna from the weekly prep (page 84)

PREP DAY:

See page 84 for the prep ingredients and instructions.

COOK NIGHT:

Remove the precooked lasagna from the refrigerator and let it stand at room temperature for 30 minutes while preheating the oven to 350°F (177°C).

Cover the lasagna with aluminum foil and bake in the oven for 20 minutes. Remove the foil and bake for an additional 5 to 10 minutes until heated through.

REHEAT NIGHT:

Remove the second precooked lasagna from the freezer and thaw completely overnight in the refrigerator.

Follow the instructions for cook night.

CRISPY BATTERED COD, SLAW AND HUSH PUPPY MUFFINS

Serves 4 on cook night and 4 on reheat night with the additional fresh ingredients found in the reheat grocery list on page 99

Fish and chips is such a classic combination. But since I didn't want an *entire* fried meal, nor you standing over your stove for two hours, I lightened it up with this bright and tangy coleslaw. Traditionally, the fish batter is made with beer, but this recipe uses sparkling water for a Paleo twist. Hush puppies, meanwhile, are a staple in the South; here I turned them into mini muffins. They're also fantastic fried if you're feeling ambitious!

COD

1½ lbs (680 g) or 4 (6-oz [170-g]) cod fillets

1 recipe batter mixture from the weekly prep (page 85)

½ to ¾ cup (120 to 180 ml) sparkling water

1 egg, gently whisked

Olive oil, for frying

1 (7.5-oz [213-g]) jar Paleo-friendly tartar sauce

COLE SLAW

⅓ cup (80 ml) apple cider vinegar

2 tbsp (30 ml) honey

1 tsp celery seeds

Salt and pepper, to taste

1 (10-oz [283-g]) bag coleslaw

1 (10-oz [283-g]) bag shredded carrots

HUSH PUPPY MINI MUFFINS

½ recipe hush puppy mini muffins from the weekly prep (page 86)

NOTE: If you'd prefer to make the sauce from scratch, see page 232 for the Tartar Sauce recipe.

PREP DAY:

See page 85 for the prep ingredients and instructions.

COOK NIGHT:

If your cod is frozen, remove the cod fillets from the freezer 1½ hours before cooking them.

Preheat the oven to 350°F (177°C).

In a large mixing bowl make the coleslaw dressing by whisking together the apple cider vinegar, honey, celery seeds, salt and pepper. Add in the coleslaw and shredded carrots and stir until they are fully coated. Set aside.

Spread the hush puppy muffins across a baking sheet and warm in the oven for about 5 minutes while the fish is frying.

Finish making the fish batter by whisking in the sparkling water and the egg.

Coat the bottom of a large skillet with the olive oil over medium-high heat.

Cut each 6-oz (170-g) fillet into two 3-oz (85-g) fillets. One by one, drop the fillets into the batter, and use a spoon to fully coat it. Add all of the battered fillets to the skillet, and cook for 3 minutes on each side. The internal temperature of your fish should be 145°F (63°C) when ready. Remove them from the heat, and immediately serve the fish with the tartar sauce, a hush puppy muffin or two and the coleslaw.

REHEAT NIGHT:

Remove the cod fillets and hush puppy muffins from the freezer 1½ hours before cooking and warming them.

Follow the remaining instructions from cook night to pull this meal together.

CRUNCHY BUFFALO CAULIFLOWER TACOS WITH A WEDGE SALAD

Serves 4 on cook night and 4 on reheat night with the additional fresh ingredients found in the reheat grocery list on page 99

These Buffalo cauliflower tacos are an explosion of flavor, and the walnuts add a ton of dimension (and protein!) to this dish. The use of store-bought Buffalo sauce and ranch dressing make this one of the fastest recipes in the entire book. My fresh Ranch Dressing recipe on page 233 is worth the added effort, though, and it's a great addition to both the salad and the tacos. Make extra for other salads or as a dip for veggies.

1 recipe Buffalo cauliflower from the weekly prep (page 87)

1 large carrot

2 ribs celery

Chopped cilantro, for topping

1 (8-piece) package taco-sized tortillas, grain free

WEDGE SALAD

1 head iceberg lettuce

1 bunch chives

1 pint (510 g) cherry tomatoes

4 slices Paleo-friendly bacon, cooked and crumbled

1 (8-oz [237-ml]) jar Paleo-friendly ranch dressing

PREP DAY:

See page 87 for the prep ingredients and instructions.

COOK NIGHT:

In a large skillet or pot over medium-high heat, add the Buffalo cauliflower and walnut mixture. Cook for 10 to 12 minutes, stirring occasionally, until the cauliflower is tender and caramelized.

While the cauliflower mixture is cooking, prep your veggies.

Slice the iceberg lettuce into four wedges, julienne the carrot and celery and roughly chop the cilantro and chives.

Serve the Buffalo taco mixture in tortillas and top with carrot, celery and cilantro. Serve with a slice of iceberg lettuce topped with cherry tomatoes, bacon bits and chives, and top with ranch dressing.

REHEAT NIGHT:

These tacos come together so quickly that there's no freeze element necessary. To remake this recipe, see page 87 for the prep ingredients and instructions. Then follow the cook night instructions to cook and serve.

NOTE: If you'd prefer to make the sauce and dressing from scratch, see page 233 for the Buffalo Sauce recipe and page 233 for the Ranch Dressing recipe.

WEEK 5 GROCERY LIST

PROTEIN
- ☐ 4 lbs (1.8 kg) ground beef ● ●
- ☐ 3½ lbs (1.6 kg) cod fillets ● ●
- ☐ 9 eggs ● ● ●
- ☐ 1 package Paleo-friendly bacon ●

PRODUCE
- ☐ 3 yellow onions ● ● ●
- ☐ 1 head garlic ● ● ●
- ☐ 1 red bell pepper ●
- ☐ 1 green bell pepper ●
- ☐ 1 yellow bell pepper ●
- ☐ 1 jalapeño ●
- ☐ 1 poblano pepper ●
- ☐ 2 large sweet potatoes ●
- ☐ 2 avocados ●
- ☐ 2 bunches cilantro ● ●
- ☐ 1 bunch radishes ●
- ☐ 2 lemons ●
- ☐ 6 ribs celery ● ●
- ☐ 2 shallots ●
- ☐ Lemon juice ●
- ☐ 2 heads romaine lettuce ●
- ☐ 1 bunch (1 cup [24 g]) basil ●
- ☐ 1 (10-oz [283-g]) bag coleslaw ●
- ☐ 1 (10-oz [283-g]) bag shredded carrots ●
- ☐ 1 head cauliflower ●
- ☐ 1 carrot ●
- ☐ 1 head iceberg lettuce ●
- ☐ 1 pint (510 g) cherry tomatoes ●
- ☐ 1 bunch chives ●

SPICES
- ☐ Chili powder ●
- ☐ Cumin ●
- ☐ Paprika ● ● ●
- ☐ Dried oregano ● ●
- ☐ Bay leaves ●
- ☐ Red pepper flakes ● ●
- ☐ Garlic salt ●
- ☐ Garlic powder ●
- ☐ Onion powder ●
- ☐ Celery seeds ●

PANTRY
- ☐ 1 (28-oz [794-g]) can diced tomatoes ●
- ☐ Paleo-friendly mayonnaise ●
- ☐ Dijon mustard ●
- ☐ Paleo-friendly bread crumbs ●
- ☐ 8 cups (1.9 L) Paleo-friendly marinara sauce (I like Primal Kitchen Tomato Basil Marinara Sauce) ●
- ☐ Tapioca starch ●
- ☐ Cassava flour ●
- ☐ ¾ cup (177 ml) unflavored sparkling water ●
- ☐ Almond flour ●
- ☐ Baking soda ●
- ☐ Monk fruit extract ●
- ☐ 1 (13.5-oz [398-ml]) can coconut milk ●
- ☐ ⅓ cup (80 ml) apple cider vinegar ●
- ☐ Honey ●
- ☐ 1 cup (117 g) walnuts ●
- ☐ 1 (8.5-oz [241-g]) jar Paleo-friendly Buffalo sauce (I like Primal Kitchen Buffalo Sauce) ●
- ☐ 1 (8-oz [237-ml]) jar Paleo-friendly ranch dressing (I like Primal Kitchen Ranch Dressing) ●
- ☐ 1 (10-oz [296-ml]) jar Paleo-friendly Caesar dressing (I like Tessemae's Organic Creamy Caesar Dressing) ●
- ☐ 1 (7.5-oz [213-g]) jar Paleo-friendly tartar sauce (I like Primal Kitchen Tartar Sauce) ●

DAIRY ALTERNATIVES

- ☐ 1 (32-oz [907-g]) container Paleo-friendly ricotta (I like Kite Hill Non-Dairy Ricotta) ●

FREEZER

- ☐ 2 (9-oz [255-g]) packages Paleo-friendly lasagna noodles (I like Cappello's Lasagna Sheets) ●
- ☐ 1 (8-piece) package taco-sized grain-free tortillas (I like Siete Cassava Tortillas) ●

RECIPES KEY: ● ● ● ● ●

Five-Pepper Sweet Potato Chili (page 88)
Lemony Cod Cakes over Caesar Salad (page 91)
Make-Ahead Homestyle Lasagna (page 92)
Crunchy Buffalo Cauliflower Tacos with a Wedge Salad (page 96)
Crispy Battered Cod, Slaw and Hush Puppy Muffins (page 95)

WEEK 5 REHEAT GROCERY LIST

FIVE-PEPPER SWEET POTATO CHILI

- ☐ 2 avocados
- ☐ 1 bunch cilantro
- ☐ 1 bunch radishes

LEMONY COD CAKES OVER CAESAR SALAD

- ☐ 1 (10-oz [296-ml]) jar Paleo-friendly Caesar dressing (I like Tessemae's Organic Creamy Caesar Dressing)
- ☐ 2 heads romaine lettuce

MAKE-AHEAD HOMESTYLE LASAGNA

- ☐ Nothing needed

CRISPY BATTERED COD, SLAW AND HUSH PUPPY MUFFINS

- ☐ 1½ lbs (680 g) or 4 (6-oz [170-g]) cod fillets
- ☐ Tapioca starch
- ☐ Cassava flour
- ☐ Paprika
- ☐ Garlic salt
- ☐ ¾ cup (177 ml) sparkling water
- ☐ 1 egg
- ☐ ⅓ cup (80 ml) apple cider vinegar
- ☐ 1 (7.5-oz [213-g]) jar Paleo-friendly tartar sauce

- ☐ Honey
- ☐ Celery seeds
- ☐ 1 (10-oz [284-g]) bag coleslaw
- ☐ 1 (10-oz [284-g]) bag shredded carrots

CRUNCHY BUFFALO CAULIFLOWER TACOS WITH A WEDGE SALAD

- ☐ 1 large head cauliflower
- ☐ 1 cup (117 g) walnuts
- ☐ 1 (8-piece) package taco-sized, grain-free tortillas
- ☐ 1 carrot
- ☐ 2 ribs celery
- ☐ 1 bunch cilantro
- ☐ 1 head iceberg lettuce
- ☐ 1 package Paleo-friendly bacon
- ☐ 1 pint (510 g) cherry tomatoes
- ☐ 1 bunch chives
- ☐ 1 (8.5-oz [241-g]) jar Paleo-friendly Buffalo sauce (I like Primal Kitchen Buffalo Sauce)
- ☐ 1 (8-oz [237-ml]) jar Paleo-friendly ranch dressing (I like Primal Kitchen Ranch Dressing)

WEEK 6

Week 6 features chicken tenderloins and ground chorizo. Chorizo is so flavorful that it takes simple recipes like a taco bowl or Bolognese to another level. But, if you don't like spicy foods, you can easily replace it with ground beef for a more family-friendly version. The creamy jalapeño sauce for the chicken tostadas could be called "the everything sauce," as we're convinced in our house that it goes well with everything. Chicken and waffles make a great breakfast for dinner, and we keep the waffle recipe as our go-to for a delicious brunch.

WEEK 6 PREP-DAY INSTRUCTIONS

Ever since I created these ultimate veggie burgers, I make them in bulk and keep them in my freezer because my kiddos love them and they're veggie-packed! That's a double win in my book. The chorizo seriously elevates the Bolognese and taco bowls without requiring any extra effort. Chicken tenderloins are such a quick protein—you'll love how fast the chicken tostadas come together. Lastly, you're going to bookmark the Paleo Fried Chicken and Waffles recipe for *both* the chicken *and* the waffles—be sure to check out the homemade waffles on page 234. Yum!

Step 1:

ULTIMATE VEGGIE BURGERS WITH KALE CHIPS

1 yellow onion, sliced

1 large sweet potato (about 2 cups [268 g]), peeled and diced

1 large carrot, cut into 1-inch (2.5-cm) pieces

1 large beet, peeled and diced

2 cloves garlic, whole

2 tbsp (30 ml) olive oil

Salt and pepper, to taste

Preheat your oven to 400°F (204°C). Line a sheet pan with parchment paper. Add the onion, sweet potato, carrot, beet and garlic, and drizzle the olive oil on top. Season with salt and pepper and toss to evenly coat the veggies. Bake in the oven for 30 to 40 minutes, until the vegetables are tender and caramelized, turning halfway through. Remove from the oven and set aside to cool.

Step 2:

CHORIZO PICCANTE ALLA BOLOGNESE

2 tbsp (30 ml) olive oil

2 tbsp (28 g) unsalted ghee

1 yellow onion, chopped (about 1 cup [160 g])

4 ribs celery, chopped

4 carrots, chopped

2 cloves garlic, minced

2 lbs (907 g) ground chorizo

Pinch of salt

Pinch of black pepper

2 tbsp (30 ml) white wine vinegar

While the veggies are baking, in a large pot over medium heat, combine the olive oil and ghee. Add the onion and cook until it is translucent, about 7 minutes. Add the celery, carrots and garlic and cook for 4 more minutes.

Bring the heat to high and add the ground chorizo, salt and pepper. Break the chorizo into small pieces with a spatula. Add the white wine vinegar. Stir occasionally until the chorizo is fully cooked, 12 to 15 minutes. The temperature should be 160°F (71°C) on an instant-read thermometer.

Step 3:

CRUNCHY CHICKEN TOSTADAS WITH A ZESTY CITRUS SAUCE

2½ lbs (1.1 kg) chicken tenderloins

1 (15-oz [425-g]) can diced tomatoes

2 tbsp (15 g) Paleo-friendly taco seasoning

While the chorizo is cooking, cook the chicken for the tostadas. If you have an Instant Pot, add the chicken, diced tomatoes and taco seasoning to it. Set the Poultry setting to 15 minutes and cook.

If you do not have an Instant Pot, combine the chicken and taco seasoning in a bowl and toss until well coated. Add the seasoned chicken and the tomatoes to a straight-sided sauté pan or Dutch oven over medium-low heat. Bring to a gentle simmer, adjusting the heat if necessary, and cook until the chicken is cooked through and tender, 7 to 10 minutes. Check the chicken using an instant-read thermometer—when the internal temperature is 165°F (74°C), remove it from the heat.

Step 4:

CHORIZO PICCANTE ALLA BOLOGNESE

¼ cup (66 g) tomato paste

2 (15-oz [425-g]) cans tomato sauce

1 tsp dried thyme

2 bay leaves

When the chorizo is fully cooked, reduce the heat to low and add the tomato paste, tomato sauce, thyme and bay leaves. Cover and simmer for 1 hour.

Step 5:

LATIN FUSION CHORIZO BOWLS

1 tbsp (15 ml) olive oil

1 yellow onion, ¼-inch (6-mm) dice

1 clove garlic, minced

2 lbs (907 g) ground chorizo

1 tbsp (7 g) chili powder

1½ tsp (3 g) ground cumin

1 tsp salt

1 tsp black pepper

½ tsp paprika

¼ tsp red pepper flakes

¼ tsp dried oregano

1 tsp coconut or almond flour

While the chorizo is simmering for the Bolognese, heat the olive oil in a large skillet over medium-high heat. Add the onion and sauté until translucent, about 3 minutes. Add the minced garlic and sauté until fragrant, about 1 more minute. Add the ground chorizo, breaking it up with a wooden spoon. Add all the seasonings and the coconut or almond flour and stir occasionally until the chorizo is fully cooked, 12 to 15 minutes. The temperature should be 160°F (71°C) on an instant-read thermometer.

Let the chorizo cool and divide into two equal portions. Store both portions in airtight containers. Place one portion in the refrigerator for cook night and the other portion in the freezer for reheat night.

Step 6:

CRUNCHY CHICKEN TOSTADAS WITH A ZESTY CITRUS SALAD

Salt and pepper, to taste

Once the chicken is fully cooked, if you used the Instant Pot, release the steam valve manually and carefully remove the chicken to a cutting board. Shred the chicken using two forks, then season to taste with salt and pepper. Divide the chicken into two equal portions, and store both portions in airtight containers. Place one portion in the refrigerator for cook night and the other portion in the freezer for reheat night.

PALEO FRIED CHICKEN AND WAFFLES

1 (12-oz [340-g]) box Paleo-friendly waffle mix

After the chicken for the tostadas is cooked, cooled and stored, you'll move onto making waffles. Follow the package instructions to make eight waffles using your store-bought Paleo-friendly waffle mix.

Set a waffle iron to a medium-high setting and generously spray with avocado oil cooking spray. Pour about ½ cup (120 ml) of batter onto the waffle iron and cook until your waffle iron says it is done, about 2 minutes. Remove the waffle and set aside to cool.

Repeat until you have eight waffles. Wrap all the waffles (in two batches of four) in parchment paper and store in an airtight container in the freezer for both cook and reheat night.

1 cup (125 g) cassava flour
¼ cup (25 g) almond flour
¼ cup (31 g) coconut flour
½ cup (64 g) tapioca starch
2 tsp (12 g) salt
2 tsp (4 g) black pepper
1 tsp cayenne pepper

While your waffles are cooking, make the flour mixture for the chicken by combining the cassava flour, almond flour, coconut flour, tapioca starch, salt, pepper and cayenne. Store in an airtight container for cook night.

ULTIMATE VEGGIE BURGERS WITH KALE CHIPS

2 ribs celery, diced
2 tbsp (32 g) tomato paste
2 tbsp (30 ml) Paleo-friendly mayonnaise
1 tbsp (15 ml) Dijon mustard
2 eggs, gently whisked
¼ cup (15 g) parsley
Pinch of red pepper flakes
½ cup (63 g) cassava flour
3 tbsp (24 g) tapioca starch
¼ cup (31 g) psyllium husks
½ cup (67 g) sunflower seeds
Salt and pepper, to taste

Once you've finished your waffles, it's time to finish up the ultimate veggie burgers. When the oven-roasted vegetables have cooled, transfer them to a large bowl and add the celery, tomato paste, mayonnaise, mustard, eggs, parsley, red pepper flakes, cassava flour, tapioca starch and psyllium husks and stir just to combine. Add half of the mixture to a food processor and pulse until the ingredients are finely chopped and fully combined. Pour the pulsed ingredients into another bowl and add the second half of the original mixture to the food processor and pulse. Add to the bowl with the other pulsed mixture, fold in the sunflower seeds and season to taste with salt and pepper.

Form eight patties and place them on a sheet pan in the refrigerator to firm up for 30 minutes.

Freeze four of the veggie burgers for reheat night. Be sure to store them in an airtight container with parchment paper between the burgers so they don't stick together.

Store the remaining four patties in the refrigerator in an airtight container with parchment paper between the burgers for cook night.

Step 9:

CHORIZO PICCANTE ALLA BOLOGNESE

1 (13.5-oz [398-ml]) can coconut milk

Once the ultimate veggie burgers are stored, you will finish up the Bolognese sauce. Add the coconut milk, cover and simmer for 30 more minutes, until the sauce has thickened.

Step 10:

CRUNCHY CHICKEN TOSTADAS WITH A ZESTY CITRUS SALAD

1 cup (240 ml) water

½ cup (120 ml) red wine vinegar

1 tbsp (15 ml) lime juice

1 tsp salt

1 tsp coconut sugar

1 red onion, thinly sliced

While the Bolognese sauce is thickening, make the pickled red onions. Add the water, vinegar, lime juice, salt and coconut sugar to a small saucepan on the stovetop. Bring to a gentle simmer, then remove from the heat. Add the sliced onion to a heatproof container and pour the warm vinegar mixture over it. Allow to cool, then cover and store in the refrigerator for up to 3 weeks.

Step 11:

CHORIZO PICCANTE ALLA BOLOGNESE

After making the pickled red onions, store the chorizo Bolognese. Allow the sauce to cool, then store half in an airtight container in the refrigerator and half in an airtight container in the freezer.

LATIN FUSION CHORIZO BOWLS

Serves 4 on cook night and 4 on reheat night with the additional fresh ingredients found in the reheat grocery list on page 117

These chorizo bowls were inspired by a local restaurant here in Denver. Chorizo is a type of pork sausage that gets its red color from paprika. It is packed with flavor and brings some heat to these taco bowls! If you've never cooked it before, trust the cook time on the package. Fried plantains are one of my all-time favorite foods and they're a great addition to this dish. For a less spicy rendition of this meal, you can substitute ground beef for the chorizo.

⅓ cup (80 g) coconut oil

4 ripe plantains, sliced on an angle

Sea salt, to taste

½ recipe cooked chorizo from the weekly prep (page 103)

1 (14-oz [397-g]) container pico de gallo

1 (7.5-oz [213-g]) container guacamole

Cilantro, for garnish (optional)

PREP DAY:

See page 103 for the prep ingredients and instructions.

COOK NIGHT:

In a large, deep skillet or Dutch oven, heat the coconut oil over medium-high heat. Working in batches, add the sliced plantains and fry until soft and golden brown, flipping halfway through, 5 to 7 minutes. Remove from the oil and rest on a plate lined with paper towels. Sprinkle with sea salt.

While you are frying your plantains, put the chorizo mixture in a pot on the stovetop and reheat over medium-high heat until warmed through, 7 to 10 minutes.

Serve the chorizo over the fried plantains and top with pico de gallo, guacamole and cilantro (if using).

REHEAT NIGHT:

Remove the chorizo mixture from the freezer and thaw overnight in the refrigerator.

Follow the instructions from cook night.

NOTE: If you'd prefer to make your pico de gallo and guacamole from scratch, see page 233 for the Pico de Gallo recipe and page 234 for the Guacamole recipe.

ULTIMATE VEGGIE BURGERS WITH KALE CHIPS

Serves 4 on cook night and 4 on reheat night with the additional fresh ingredients found in the reheat grocery list on page 117

For years now, I have wanted to create the ultimate veggie burgers—a recipe that I would want to make over and over again that my kids would like even though it's entirely vegetables. This cookbook was the catalyst for doing just that. You will be impressed with how many vegetables are in these burgers and that your whole family will enjoy them!

KALE CHIPS
1 head kale

3 tbsp (45 ml) olive oil or coconut oil, divided

Sea salt

BURGERS
½ recipe veggie burgers from the weekly prep (page 102)

1 tbsp (15 ml) olive oil

1 head Bibb lettuce

PREP DAY:
See page 102 for the prep ingredients and instructions.

COOK NIGHT:
Preheat the oven to 300°F (149°C).

Remove the ribs from the kale leaves and cut or shred the leaves into bite-sized pieces. Spread the kale across a sheet pan, then drizzle 2 tablespoons (30 ml) of oil on top and sprinkle with sea salt. Using your hands, toss until the kale is well coated. Bake until the leaves are crispy, about 20 minutes, turning halfway through.

While the kale chips are baking, remove the four veggie patties from the refrigerator. In a large skillet over medium heat, heat the olive oil. Place the veggie patties in the skillet and sauté 4 to 5 minutes per side, or until browned and fully cooked.

Serve your veggie burgers on a Bibb lettuce "bun" with your favorite burger toppings and kale chips on the side.

REHEAT NIGHT:
Remove the veggie patties from the freezer and thaw overnight in the refrigerator.

Follow the instructions for cook night.

CRUNCHY CHICKEN TOSTADAS WITH A ZESTY CITRUS SALAD

Serves 4 on cook night and 4 on reheat night with the additional fresh ingredients found in the reheat grocery list on page 117

A tostada uses a crispy tortilla as the base for other delicious toppings. These tostadas are made particularly tasty because of their toppings: pickled red onions and the creamy jalapeño sauce, which is absolutely worth making from scratch (page 233). Then everything is lightened up with a fresh and bright avocado-citrus salad that reminds me of sunny summer days.

½ recipe chicken from the weekly prep (page 102)

ZESTY CITRUS SALAD

2 tbsp (30 g) pickled red onions from the weekly prep (page 105)

2 tbsp (30 ml) olive oil

1 tbsp (15 ml) lime juice

Salt and pepper, to taste

1 tsp honey

1 grapefruit, peeled and sliced or segmented

1 orange, peeled and sliced or segmented

1 lemon, peeled and sliced or segmented

1 avocado, sliced

FOR SERVING

4 tbsp (59 ml) olive oil

1 (8-piece) package taco-sized grain-free tortillas

1 head lettuce, shredded, for topping

2 tomatoes, diced, for topping

1 (10-oz [296-ml]) jar Paleo-friendly spicy ranch dressing

Extra pickled red onions from the weekly prep (page 105)

PREP DAY:

See page 102 for the prep ingredients and instructions.

COOK NIGHT:

Remove the chicken and pickled red onions from the refrigerator.

Make the zesty citrus salad by combining the olive oil, lime juice, salt and pepper and honey in a small bowl and whisking together to make the dressing. Add the citrus, avocado and pickled onions to a serving bowl, add the dressing and toss to coat. Set aside.

In a pot on the stovetop over medium heat, reheat the chicken, stirring occasionally, until warmed through, 8 to 10 minutes.

While the chicken is reheating, pour the olive oil into a shallow skillet and heat over medium-high heat. Once the oil is hot, add the tortillas one or two at a time and fry until crispy, 30 seconds to 1 minute per side.

Build your tostadas by adding the chicken, lettuce, tomatoes, ranch dressing and pickled red onions, then serve with the zesty citrus salad.

REHEAT NIGHT:

Remove the chicken from the freezer and thaw overnight in the refrigerator.

Follow the instructions for cook night.

NOTE: If you'd prefer to make the tostadas using homemade taco seasoning and sauce, see page 231 for the Taco Seasoning recipe and page 233 for the Creamy Jalapeño Sauce recipe.

PALEO FRIED CHICKEN AND WAFFLES

Serves 4 on cook night and 4 on reheat night with the additional fresh ingredients found in the reheat grocery list on page 117

Does this recipe even need an introduction? Chicken and waffles is such a classic combination. Plus, who doesn't love breakfast for dinner? On a leisurely weekend, be sure to make the home-made waffles found on page 234—you'll dog-ear that page to make the perfect brunch waffles over and over again. Even without the waffles, you can make these fried chicken–style chicken fingers that are kid-approved any time—simply make them ahead and freeze them for a quick lunch or dinner.

1 (15-oz [425-g]) can coconut milk

2 tbsp (30 ml) lemon juice

2½ tsp (15 g) salt, divided

2½ tsp (7 g) black pepper, divided

2 eggs, gently whisked

1½ lbs (680 g) chicken tenderloins

Flour mixture from the weekly prep (page 104)

3 tbsp (45 ml) avocado oil, for frying

3 tbsp (45 ml) olive oil, for frying

4 waffles from the weekly prep (page 104)

½ cup (120 ml) maple syrup, for serving (optional)

NOTE: If you'd prefer to make the waffles from scratch, see page 234.

PREP DAY:

See page 104 for the prep ingredients and instructions.

COOK NIGHT:

In a shallow dish, mix together the coconut milk, lemon juice, ½ teaspoon of salt, ½ teaspoon of pepper and the eggs. Soak the chicken tenderloins in the coconut milk mixture for 1 hour.

Meanwhile, transfer the flour mixture from the weekly prep to a separate shallow dish and set aside.

Preheat the oven to 425°F (218°C).

Once the chicken has soaked in the coconut mixture, heat the avocado and olive oils in a large cast-iron skillet. Once the oils are hot, working in batches, dredge the chicken tenderloins through the flour mixture and fry them in the oil for 8 to 10 minutes, flipping halfway through, until they're golden brown or an instant-read thermometer reads 165°F (74°C).

Remove the chicken from the oil and set it on a towel or paper towel–lined plate to absorb the excess oil.

Remove four waffles from the freezer and place them on a wire rack over a sheet pan. Spray them with cooking oil and place the sheet pan in the oven to reheat for 3 to 5 minutes, until warmed through and crispy.

Serve the chicken on top of the waffles and drizzle with maple syrup, if desired.

REHEAT NIGHT:

Follow the instructions for cook night.

CHORIZO PICCANTE ALLA BOLOGNESE

Serves 4 on cook night and 4 on reheat night with the additional fresh ingredients found in the reheat grocery list on page 117

Bolognese is a slowly cooked meat ragù sauce served over pasta. This dish is a great way to sneak some veggies into a traditional pasta sauce. Using ground chorizo makes this dish an even more flavorful and spicy rendition. You will love how quickly this meal comes together thanks to the work you did on prep day. You're basically just boiling water for pasta and heating up the sauce! It's a flavor-packed, easy weeknight meal. For less spice, you can substitute ground beef for the chorizo.

½ recipe chorizo piccante alla Bolognese from the weekly prep (page 102)

1 (9-oz [255-g]) box Paleo-friendly noodles

PREP DAY:

See page 102 for the prep ingredients and instructions.

COOK NIGHT:

Remove the Bolognese sauce from the refrigerator and add it to a large pot over medium heat. Heat until warmed through while your pasta is cooking, about 10 minutes.

Cook your pasta according to the package instructions. Serve the warmed sauce over the pasta.

REHEAT NIGHT:

To thaw the Bolognese overnight, move it from the freezer to the refrigerator the night before reheat night. To thaw day of, move the container from the freezer to your countertop and allow the Bolognese to completely thaw at room temperature. For a quick thaw, submerge the container in room temperature water until completely thawed. Once thawed, use the instructions from cook night to bring this meal together.

WEEK 6 GROCERY LIST

PROTEIN
- ☐ 4 eggs ● ●
- ☐ 4 lbs (1.8 kg) chicken tenderloins ● ●
- ☐ 4 lbs (1.8 kg) ground chorizo ● ●

PRODUCE
- ☐ 3 yellow onions ● ● ●
- ☐ 1 large sweet potato ●
- ☐ 5 carrots ● ●
- ☐ 1 beet ●
- ☐ 1 head garlic ● ● ●
- ☐ 1 bunch celery ● ●
- ☐ 1 bunch flat-leaf parsley ●
- ☐ 1 red onion ●
- ☐ Lime juice ●
- ☐ 1 grapefruit ●
- ☐ 1 orange ●
- ☐ 1 lemon ●
- ☐ 1 avocado ●
- ☐ 2 tomatoes ●
- ☐ 1 head lettuce ●
- ☐ Lemon juice ●
- ☐ 4 plantains ●
- ☐ 2 bunches cilantro ●
- ☐ 1 head kale ●
- ☐ 1 head Bibb lettuce ●

SPICES
- ☐ Red pepper flakes ● ●
- ☐ Chili powder ●
- ☐ Cumin ●
- ☐ Paprika ●
- ☐ Dried oregano ●
- ☐ Cayenne ●
- ☐ Dried thyme ●
- ☐ Bay leaves ●
- ☐ Taco seasoning (I like Siete Taco Seasoning) ●

PANTRY
- ☐ 1 (6-oz [170-g]) can tomato paste ● ●
- ☐ Paleo-friendly mayonnaise ●

- ☐ Dijon mustard ●
- ☐ Cassava flour ● ●
- ☐ Tapioca starch ● ●
- ☐ ¼ cup (31 g) psyllium husks ●
- ☐ ½ cup (67 g) sunflower seeds ●
- ☐ 1 (15-oz [425-g]) can diced tomatoes ●
- ☐ Almond flour ●
- ☐ ½ cup (120 ml) red wine vinegar ●
- ☐ Coconut sugar ●
- ☐ Honey ●
- ☐ 2 (13.5-oz [398-ml]) cans coconut milk ● ●
- ☐ Coconut flour ● ●
- ☐ Avocado oil ●
- ☐ ⅓ cup (80 g) coconut oil ●
- ☐ Maple syrup ●
- ☐ White wine vinegar ●
- ☐ 2 (15-oz [425-g]) cans tomato sauce ●
- ☐ 1 (9-oz [255-g]) box Paleo-friendly pasta noodles (I like Cappello's Fettuccine) ●
- ☐ 1 (12-oz [340-g]) box Paleo-friendly waffle mix (I like Birch Benders Paleo Pancake & Waffle Mix) ●
- ☐ 1 (10-oz [296-ml]) jar Paleo-friendly spicy ranch dressing (I like Tessemae's Organic Habanero Ranch Dressing) ●
- ☐ 1 (14-oz [397-g]) container pico de gallo ●
- ☐ 1 (7.5-oz [213-g]) container guacamole ●

DAIRY ALTERNATIVES
- ☐ Unsalted ghee (I like Fourth & Heart) ●

FREEZER
- ☐ 1 (8-piece) package taco-sized grain-free tortillas (I like Siete Cassava Tortillas) ●

RECIPES KEY: ● ● ● ● ●

Latin Fusion Chorizo Bowls (page 106)
Crunchy Chicken Tostadas with a Zesty Citrus Salad (page 110)
Chorizo Piccante alla Bolognese (page 114)
Ultimate Veggie Burgers with Kale Chips (page 109)
Paleo Fried Chicken and Waffles (page 113)

WEEK 6 REHEAT GROCERY LIST

LATIN FUSION CHORIZO BOWLS

- ☐ ⅓ cup (80 g) coconut oil
- ☐ 4 ripe plantains
- ☐ 1 (14-oz [397-g]) container pico de gallo
- ☐ 1 (7.5-oz [213-g]) container guacamole
- ☐ 1 bunch cilantro

ULTIMATE VEGGIE BURGERS WITH KALE CHIPS

- ☐ 1 head kale
- ☐ 1 head Bibb lettuce

CRUNCHY CHICKEN TOSTADAS WITH A ZESTY CITRUS SALAD

- ☐ 1 grapefruit
- ☐ 1 orange
- ☐ 1 lemon
- ☐ 1 avocado
- ☐ Lime juice
- ☐ Honey
- ☐ 1 (8-piece) package taco-sized grain-free tortillas (I like Siete Cassava Tortillas)
- ☐ 1 head lettuce
- ☐ 2 tomatoes
- ☐ 1 (10-oz [296-ml]) jar spicy ranch dressing (I like Tessemae's Organic Habanero Ranch Dressing)

PALEO FRIED CHICKEN AND WAFFLES

- ☐ 1 (13.5-oz [398-ml]) can coconut milk
- ☐ Lemon juice
- ☐ 2 eggs
- ☐ 1½ lbs (680 g) chicken tenderloins
- ☐ Cassava flour
- ☐ Almond flour
- ☐ Coconut flour
- ☐ Tapioca starch
- ☐ Cayenne pepper
- ☐ Avocado oil
- ☐ Maple syrup

CHORIZO PICCANTE ALLA BOLOGNESE

- ☐ 1 (9-oz [255-g]) box Paleo-friendly noodles

WEEK 7

Mexican and Italian cuisines are hands down my two favorites, and this week is the perfect combination of both! Week 7 features shrimp and turkey breast. These two shrimp recipes are so easy and will give you a nice kick! For the turkey recipes, if you can't find or don't enjoy turkey breast, you can easily swap it for chicken breast. My friend made the pot pie and reported back that her fiancé said it was the best thing she had ever made for him. It freezes perfectly, so it's easy to thaw and cook with no hands-on time at all.

WEEK 7 PREP-DAY INSTRUCTIONS

I absolutely love sun-dried tomatoes, and you will want to use them in as many recipes as possible after making this bruschetta turkey! The turkey pot pie is another dish you're going to make often to keep as a frozen back-up option. Ratatouille is delicious, but recipes for it usually take a *ton* of meticulous time. This Deconstructed Ratatouille Pasta gives you all of the flavor but with way less work and in just a fraction of the time. Lastly, I love the shrimp recipes because they are so quick and easy!

Step 1:

SUN-DRIED TOMATO BRUSCHETTA TURKEY WITH ROASTED BROCCOLINI

2 lbs (907 g) turkey breast

½ cup (27 g) sun-dried tomato bruschetta mix

1 tsp kosher salt

1 clove garlic, minced

1 tsp black pepper (if not using Instant Pot)

2 tbsp (30 ml) olive oil (if not using Instant Pot)

To make the bruschetta turkey, add the turkey, bruschetta mix, salt and garlic to the Instant Pot. Set the Instant Pot to the Poultry setting and cook for 20 minutes.

If you do not have an Instant Pot, preheat the oven to 400°F (204°C). Heat a large cast-iron skillet or Dutch oven over medium heat. Season the turkey breast with the salt and pepper and pour the olive oil into the pan. Add the turkey and brown it on each side, 3 to 4 minutes per side. Add the bruschetta mix and minced garlic. Remove the pan from the stovetop, cover it with a lid and place it in the oven for 40 to 45 minutes until the internal temperature of the turkey reaches 165°F (74°C). Remove the turkey from the oven.

Step 2:

CLASSIC TURKEY POT PIE

PIE CRUST

4 cups (500 g) cassava flour

1 cup (95 g) almond flour

½ cup (63 g) coconut flour

2 cups (256 g) tapioca starch

1 tsp xanthan gum

4 tsp (24 g) salt

2 cups (454 g) unsalted ghee, cold

12 egg yolks

1½ cups (360 ml) ice water

While your bruschetta turkey is cooking, make your pie dough in a large stand mixer. Add the cassava, almond and coconut flours; the tapioca starch; xanthan gum and salt to the mixing bowl and using the beater attachment, mix to combine on low speed.

Cut the ghee into a small dice and add it to the flour mixture. Beat on a low setting until the mixture is crumbly. Next add your egg yolks a few at a time until all have been added. Continue to beat on low and drizzle in the ice water a few tablespoons (45 ml) at a time until the dough begins to come together.

Remove the dough from the mixer and divide it into four equal portions. Wrap each portion tightly in plastic wrap and place in the refrigerator to cool.

Step 3:

SUN-DRIED TOMATO BRUSCHETTA TURKEY WITH ROASTED BROCCOLINI

If you cooked the turkey in the Instant Pot, once it's done, manually release the pressure.

Once the turkey is cool enough to handle, transfer it to a cutting board, shred it with two forks and divide the turkey into two equal portions. Place both portions into airtight containers. Store one portion in the refrigerator for cook night and the other portion in the freezer for reheat night.

Step 4:

CLASSIC TURKEY POT PIE

POT PIE FILLING

⅓ cup (80 g) ghee

1 onion, chopped

3 carrots, cut in ¼-inch (6-mm) circles

3 ribs celery, chopped into small pieces

2 russet potatoes, peeled and cut into ½-inch (1.3-cm) dice

1 clove garlic, minced

2 tbsp (16 g) arrowroot

½ cup (120 ml) chicken bone broth

½ cup (120 ml) coconut milk

1 tsp fresh thyme

1 tsp fresh parsley

2 lbs (907 g) turkey breasts, cut into ½-inch (1.3-cm) cubes

1 cup (134 g) frozen peas

1 tbsp (18 g) salt

1 tsp black pepper

After you have stored the bruschetta turkey, it's time to make the filling for the pot pies. Put the ghee in a soup pot over medium-high heat. Add the onion, carrots, celery and potatoes and cook, stirring occasionally, for 10 minutes or until the carrots and potatoes begin to get tender. Add the garlic and cook until fragrant, about 1 minute more.

Add the arrowroot and mix well until the veggies are coated.

Add the chicken bone broth, coconut milk, thyme and parsley. Bring the mixture to a boil, then add the turkey and stir. Reduce the heat to medium and simmer until the turkey is cooked through, about 10 minutes. Add the peas, salt and pepper and stir to combine. Remove the pot pie filling from the heat and set aside to cool.

While the filling is cooling, assemble the two pies. Preheat the oven to 425°F (218°C) and remove the pie dough from the refrigerator. One by one, roll out each pie crust between two sheets of parchment paper. Fit each pie crust into a standard 9-inch (23-cm) pie pan and then fill each dish with half of the turkey filling. Cover each pie with the remaining pie crust, trimming and crimping the edges. Cut multiple slits along the top of the crust to allow the steam to escape.

Bake both pies in the oven for 30 to 40 minutes or until the top is crunchy.

Step 5:

DECONSTRUCTED RATATOUILLE PASTA

¼ cup (60 ml) olive oil, divided

1 medium eggplant, cut into ½-inch (1.3-cm) dice

1 yellow squash, cut into ¾-inch (2-cm) dice

1 zucchini, cut into ¾-inch (2-cm) dice

4 Roma tomatoes, cut into ¾-inch (2-cm) dice

Start making the ratatouille pasta by cooking the vegetables. In a Dutch oven over medium heat, heat 2 tablespoons (30 ml) of olive oil. Add the eggplant and sauté until soft and golden brown, 5 to 7 minutes. Remove the eggplant from the pot and set it aside. Pour the remaining 2 tablespoons (30 ml) of olive oil into the pot and add the diced squash, zucchini and tomatoes. Sauté until all the vegetables are tender and turning golden brown, 5 to 7 minutes. Return the eggplant to the pot and remove the pot from the heat.

SAUCE

2 tbsp (30 ml) olive oil

1 yellow onion, diced

1 red bell pepper, diced

1 yellow bell pepper, diced

2 cloves garlic, minced

½ tsp red pepper flakes

2 (24-oz [680-g]) jars Paleo-friendly marinara sauce

6 tbsp (9 g) basil, chopped, divided

Salt and pepper, to taste

While the vegetables are cooking, make the sauce. In a large pot, heat the olive oil over medium heat and add the onion. Sauté the onion until translucent, 3 to 5 minutes. Add the red and yellow bell peppers and sauté until soft, about 5 minutes. Add the garlic and red pepper flakes and sauté until fragrant, about 1 minute more.

Add both jars of marinara sauce and stir to combine. Remove the pot from the heat and stir in the chopped basil. Season to taste with salt and pepper.

Once the sauce has cooled, gently stir in the cooked ratatouille vegetables and divide the sauce and vegetables into two equal portions. Place each portion in an airtight container. Store one portion in the refrigerator for cook night and the other portion in the freezer for reheat night.

Step 6:

CLASSIC TURKEY POT PIE

Remove the pot pies from the oven when the tops are golden. Allow both pies to completely cool. Cover both pies with plastic wrap and then aluminum foil. Place one pie in the refrigerator for cook night and the other pie in the freezer for reheat night.

DECONSTRUCTED RATATOUILLE PASTA

Serves 4 on cook night and 4 on reheat night with the additional fresh ingredients found in the reheat grocery list on page 135

Ratatouille is an herbed, stewed vegetable dish. If you have the time, it is quite fun to put all of the round vegetables into a round dish. But when you don't have the time, turn to this recipe! With this pasta, you get all of the flavors without all of the fuss. The extra vegetables in this sauce pair perfectly with the sautéed vegetables, and since you're making the vegetables on prep day, it's a breeze to pull together!

2 (8-oz [227-g]) boxes Paleo-friendly spaghetti noodles

½ recipe sauce and vegetables for ratatouille from the weekly prep (page 123)

PREP DAY:

See page 123 for the prep ingredients and instructions.

COOK NIGHT:

Bring a large pot of water to a boil on the stovetop and cook the pasta according to the package directions.

While the pasta is cooking, remove the sauce and vegetables from the refrigerator and add them to a pot over medium heat. Bring to a gentle simmer and, when the pasta is cooked and drained, add the pasta to the sauce and stir to combine.

REHEAT NIGHT:

To thaw the vegetables and sauce overnight, move them from the freezer to the refrigerator the night before reheat night. To thaw day of, move each container from the freezer to your countertop and allow the vegetables and sauce to completely thaw at room temperature. For a quick thaw, submerge each container in room temperature water until completely thawed. Once thawed, follow all of the instructions for cook night.

EASY SHEET PAN SHRIMP FAJITAS

Serves 4 on cook night and 4 on reheat night with the additional fresh ingredients found in the reheat grocery list on page 135

Fajitas are a great choice for the Paleo diet because they're made with meat and veggies. I've taken an already easy meal and made it even easier by transforming it into a sheet pan meal, which means your only true hands-on time is chopping veggies. Getting a store-bought fajita seasoning trims time off this recipe even more. You can use your favorite sliced protein here in place of the shrimp.

1½ lbs (680 g) wild caught shrimp, peeled and deveined

1 yellow bell pepper, thinly sliced

1 orange bell pepper, thinly sliced

1 red bell pepper, thinly sliced

1 red onion, thinly sliced

1 clove garlic, minced

2 tbsp (30 ml) olive oil

2 tbsp (15 g) fajita seasoning

1 bunch cilantro, chopped

Juice of 1 lime

1 (8-piece) package taco-sized grain-free tortillas

2 avocados, mashed

PREP DAY:

This recipe comes together so quickly on cook night that there's nothing to do on prep day!

COOK NIGHT:

Preheat the oven to 450°F (232°C).

In a large bowl, combine the shrimp, bell peppers, red onion, garlic, olive oil and fajita seasoning. Toss to coat.

Line a sheet pan with aluminum foil and spread the shrimp and vegetables across it.

Bake in the oven for 8 to 10 minutes, until the vegetables are tender and the shrimp is cooked through. Turn the oven to broil and heat under the broiler for an additional 2 to 4 minutes, until the shrimp and vegetables have an additional char to your taste.

Remove from the oven and garnish with chopped cilantro and a squeeze of lime juice. Serve in warm tortillas with mashed avocado.

REHEAT NIGHT:

Follow the instructions for cook night.

NOTE: If you'd prefer to make the fajita seasoning from scratch, see page 234 for the recipe. You can use it over and over again.

SUN-DRIED TOMATO BRUSCHETTA TURKEY WITH ROASTED BROCCOLINI

Serves 4 on cook night and 4 on reheat night with the additional fresh ingredients found in the reheat grocery list on page 135

What did I tell you? I adore sun-dried tomatoes. And before you get after me for calling this recipe bruschetta turkey, I know. The term "bruschetta" refers to the *toast* and not the tomato topping . . . but you knew what I was talking about, didn't you? This recipe changed up the traditional bruschetta topping with sun-dried tomatoes, and now I'll never make it without them! Use the homemade version of this sun-dried tomato bruschetta (page 234) on Paleo toasts for a great appetizer!

You can replace the turkey breast with chicken breast if you prefer.

2 bunches broccolini

2 tbsp (30 ml) olive oil

Pinch of red pepper flakes

Salt and pepper, to taste

½ recipe turkey from the weekly prep (page 120)

2 Roma tomatoes, diced

1 bunch basil, sliced

2 tbsp (16 g) pine nuts

1 tsp lemon juice

PREP DAY:

See page 120 for the prep ingredients and instructions.

COOK NIGHT:

Preheat the oven to 400°F (204°C).

Trim the broccolini and combine with the olive oil and red pepper flakes, then season with salt and pepper. Spread across a sheet pan and roast in the oven for 15 to 20 minutes until tender and starting to brown, tossing midway through.

While the broccolini is roasting, reheat the turkey mixture in a shallow skillet over medium-low heat for 5 to 7 minutes. Once warmed through, remove from the heat and toss in the diced tomatoes and sliced basil. Season to taste with salt and pepper.

Once the broccolini is cooked, spoon it into a serving bowl. Toss in the pine nuts and lemon juice, then serve it with the bruschetta turkey.

REHEAT NIGHT:

Remove the turkey from the freezer and thaw completely.

Follow the instructions for cook night.

NOTE: If you'd prefer to make the sun-dried tomato bruschetta from scratch, see page 234 for the recipe.

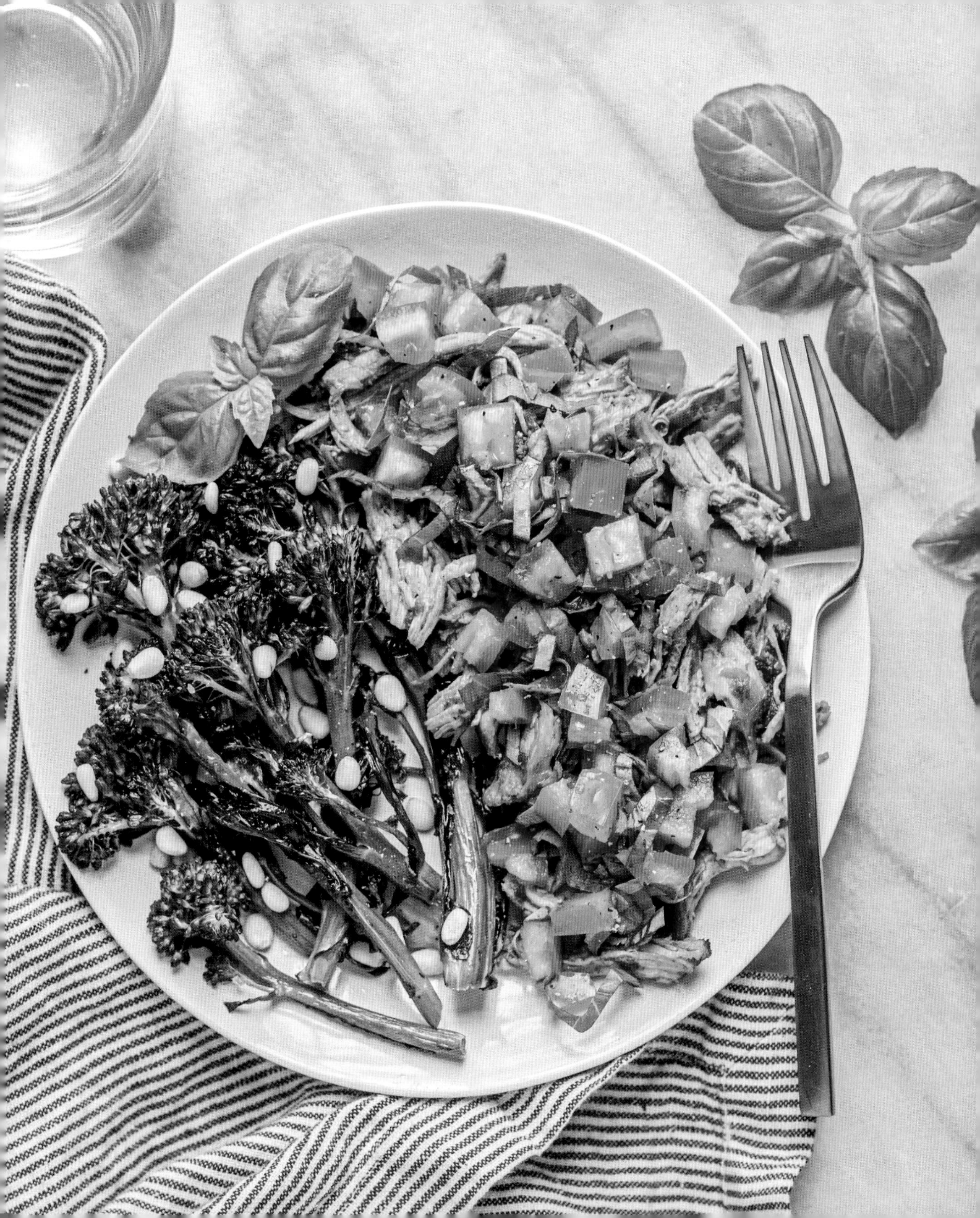

SPICY SHRIMP DIABLO OVER ZOODLES

Serves 4 on cook night and 4 on reheat night with the additional fresh ingredients found in the reheat grocery list on page 135

This "devil shrimp" recipe gets its name because of the kick! The sauce for this Mexican pasta dish is made primarily with tomatoes and chiles. If you're not a huge fan of heat and you're making the Diablo sauce from scratch (see page 235), start without the arbol and guajillo chiles, and add in a little bit at a time until it reaches your desired heat level. I like to use zoodles, but feel free to use your favorite Paleo-friendly noodles instead.

1 (24-oz [680-g]) jar Paleo-friendly diablo sauce

1 to 1½ lbs (454 to 680 g) shrimp, peeled, deveined and tails removed

1 tbsp (15 ml) lime or lemon juice

Salt and pepper, to taste

2 zucchini, spiralized into zoodles or 2 (8-oz [227-g]) packages pre-cut zoodles

1 tbsp (15 ml) olive oil (if sautéing zoodles)

2 tbsp (3 g) fresh parsley, chopped, for garnish

PREP DAY:

This recipe comes together so quickly that there's no prep element!

COOK NIGHT:

Add the diablo sauce to a straight-sided sauté pan and bring it to a gentle simmer over medium heat. Add the shrimp and simmer, uncovered, for an additional 5 to 7 minutes or until the shrimp are cooked through. Remove the pan from the heat and stir in the lime or lemon juice. Season to taste with salt and pepper.

You can serve this with raw or sautéed zoodles. To sauté the zoodles, heat the olive oil in a large skillet over medium heat. Add the zoodles and sauté until tender, 3 to 5 minutes. Serve with the diablo sauce and shrimp and garnish with chopped parsley.

REHEAT NIGHT:

Follow the instructions for cook night.

NOTE: If you'd prefer to make the sauce from scratch, see page 235 for the Diablo Sauce recipe.

CLASSIC TURKEY POT PIE

Serves 4 on cook night and 4 on reheat night

I don't think it gets any better than a pot pie. While I think of it as a Southern staple, the concept of a pot pie actually goes all the way back to Greece! There are tons of variations of meats and vegetables, but this mouthwatering and comforting rendition is a Paleo version of the American classic you likely know and love. You can replace the turkey breast with chicken breast if you'd prefer.

1 pot pie from the weekly prep (pages 120 and 121)

PREP DAY:

See pages 120 and 121 for the prep ingredients and instructions.

COOK NIGHT:

Remove the pot pie from the refrigerator and let it stand at room temperature for 30 minutes while preheating the oven to 350°F (177°C). Remove the aluminum foil and the plastic wrap and then use the same foil to wrap the edges of the pie so they won't burn.

Place the pie in the warmed oven and reheat it for 20 to 30 minutes, rotating halfway through.

REHEAT NIGHT:

To thaw the pot pie, move it from the freezer to the refrigerator the night before reheat night to give it adequate time to completely thaw. Once thawed, follow the instructions from cook night.

WEEK 7 GROCERY LIST

PROTEIN

- ☐ 3 lbs (1.4 kg) wild-caught shrimp ● ●
- ☐ 4 lbs (1.8 kg) turkey breast ● ●
- ☐ 12 eggs ●

PRODUCE

- ☐ 1 eggplant ●
- ☐ 1 yellow squash ●
- ☐ 5 zucchini (or 1 zucchini plus 3 [8-oz (227-g)] packages pre-cut zoodles) ● ●
- ☐ 6 Roma tomatoes ● ●
- ☐ 2 yellow onions ● ●
- ☐ 2 red bell peppers ● ●
- ☐ 1 head garlic ● ● ● ●
- ☐ 2 bunches basil ● ●
- ☐ 2 yellow bell peppers ● ●
- ☐ 1 orange bell pepper ●
- ☐ 1 red onion ●
- ☐ 1 bunch cilantro ●
- ☐ 2 avocados ●
- ☐ 1 lime ●
- ☐ 2 bunches broccolini ●
- ☐ Lemon juice ● ●
- ☐ 1 bunch flat-leaf parsley ● ●
- ☐ 3 carrots ●
- ☐ 3 ribs celery ●
- ☐ 2 russet potatoes ●
- ☐ 1 bunch thyme ●

SPICES

- ☐ Red pepper flakes ● ●
- ☐ 2 tbsp (15 g) fajita seasoning (I like Balanced Bites Taco & Fajita Spice Blend) ●

PANTRY

- ☐ 2 (24-oz [680-g]) jars Paleo-friendly marinara sauce ●
- ☐ 2 (8-oz [227-g]) boxes Paleo-friendly spaghetti noodles ●
- ☐ 2 tbsp (16 g) pine nuts ●
- ☐ 1 (32-oz [960-ml]) box chicken bone broth ●
- ☐ Cassava flour ●
- ☐ Almond flour ●
- ☐ Coconut flour ●
- ☐ Tapioca starch ●
- ☐ Xanthan gum ●
- ☐ Arrowroot ●
- ☐ 1 (13.5-oz [398-ml]) can coconut milk ●
- ☐ 1 (10-oz [284-g]) jar bruschetta mix (I like DeLallo Sun-Dried Tomato Bruschetta) ●
- ☐ 1 (24-oz [680-g]) jar Paleo-friendly diablo sauce (I like Rao's Arrabbiata Sauce) ●

DAIRY ALTERNATIVES

- ☐ 2⅔ cups (631 g) unsalted ghee (I like Fourth & Heart) ●

FREEZER

- ☐ 1 (8-piece) package taco-sized grain-free tortillas (I like Siete Cassava Tortillas) ●
- ☐ 1 cup (134 g) frozen peas ●

RECIPES KEY: ● ● ● ● ●

Easy Sheet Pan Shrimp Fajitas (page 127)
Sun-Dried Tomato Bruschetta Turkey with Roasted Broccolini (page 128)
Spicy Shrimp Diablo over Zoodles (page 131)
Deconstructed Ratatouille Pasta (page 124)
Classic Turkey Pot Pie (page 132)

DECONSTRUCTED RATATOUILLE PASTA

☐ 1 (16-oz [454-g]) box Paleo-friendly pasta

EASY SHEET PAN SHRIMP FAJITAS

☐ 1½ lbs (680 g) wild caught shrimp

☐ 2 tbsp (15 g) fajita seasoning (I like Balanced Bites Taco & Fajita Spice Blend)

☐ 1 yellow bell pepper

☐ 1 orange bell pepper

☐ 1 red bell pepper

☐ 1 red onion

☐ 1 clove garlic

☐ 1 bunch cilantro

☐ 1 (8-piece) package taco-sized grain-free tortillas (I like Siete Cassava Tortillas)

☐ 2 avocados

☐ 1 lime

SUN-DRIED TOMATO BRUSCHETTA TURKEY WITH ROASTED BROCCOLINI

☐ 2 bunches broccolini

☐ Red pepper flakes

☐ 2 Roma tomatoes

☐ 1 bunch basil

☐ 2 tbsp (16 g) pine nuts

☐ Lemon juice

SPICY SHRIMP DIABLO OVER ZOODLES

☐ 1½ lbs (680 g) shrimp

☐ 2 zucchini or 1 package pre-cut zoodles

☐ Lemon juice

☐ 1 bunch flat-leaf parsley

☐ 1 (24-oz [680-g]) jar Paleo-friendly diablo sauce (I like Rao's Arrabbiata Sauce)

CLASSIC TURKEY POT PIE

☐ Nothing needed

WEEK 8

Tacos with Feta Slaw (page 142)

Root Veggie Bowls (page 145)

eja with Fried Plantains (page 146)

oppyseed Casserole (page 149)

Thai Basil Beef over Coconut Cauliflower Rice (page 150)

This week's meals encompass a wide range of cuisines: American, Greek, Cuban and Thai. The roasted root veggie bowls are such a flavorful and filling vegetarian meal, and if you've never had Chicken Poppyseed Casserole, a Southern favorite, you will adore my Paleo version. It is the ultimate comfort food! And the ropa vieja is a win-win because it is as delicious as it is popular with kiddos.

WEEK 8 PREP-DAY INSTRUCTIONS

This prep day you'll be incorporating a lot of different cooking methods—"cooking on all four burners," as my mother would say! You will roast veggies in the oven, bake the Chicken Poppyseed Casserole in the oven, make the ropa vieja in the Instant Pot (or on the stovetop), and make the Thai Basil Beef in a wok or skillet. The Smoky Ropa Vieja is potentially the easiest recipe in the entire book, and my kiddos specifically ask for it!

Step 1:

VIBRANT ROASTED ROOT VEGGIE BOWLS

Preheat the oven to 400°F (204°C).

Step 2:

CHICKEN POPPYSEED CASSEROLE

2 lbs (907 g) boneless, skinless chicken breasts

1 to 2 cups (240 to 480 ml) water (depending on whether you're using the Instant Pot or stovetop)

Salt and pepper (if using the Instant Pot)

4 tsp (10 g) kosher salt (if using the stovetop)

To make the Chicken Poppyseed Casserole, first cook the chicken breasts in an Instant Pot. Add 1 cup (240 ml) of water to the bottom of the Instant Pot and add the trivet to the bottom. Place the chicken breasts on top of the trivet and season with salt and pepper. Set the Instant Pot to Pressure Cook High for 10 minutes (for thawed chicken breasts) or 15 minutes (for frozen chicken breasts).

If you do not have an Instant Pot, poaching the chicken breasts on the stovetop is a quick and easy way to get cooked, juicy chicken for your casserole.

Place the chicken breasts in a large straight-sided sauté pan or pot on the stovetop. Add 2 cups (480 ml) of cold water per breast. Season with the kosher salt. Turn the heat to medium and bring the water to a gentle boil. As soon as the water comes to a boil, turn the chicken breasts over, cover the pan and remove it from the heat. The chicken will continue to cook in the hot water. Check the chicken in about 7 minutes—when their internal temperature reaches 165°F (74°C) on an instant-read thermometer, transfer them from the water to a cutting board.

Step 3:

VIBRANT ROASTED ROOT VEGGIE BOWLS

2 heads cauliflower, outer leaves removed and chopped into bite-sized pieces

4 sweet potatoes, peeled and ½-inch (1.3-cm) dice

2 large golden beets, peeled and ½-inch (1.3-cm) dice

½ cup (120 ml) olive oil, divided

Salt and pepper, to taste

While the chicken breasts are cooking, arrange all the chopped vegetables between two or three sheet pans. (Be careful not to crowd the vegetables or they will steam instead of roast. If you don't have three sheet pans or three oven racks, you can do this step in batches.) Drizzle the olive oil over the vegetables and season with salt and pepper.

Roast the vegetables in the preheated oven until tender and golden, about 45 minutes, turning halfway through the cook time.

Step 4:

CHICKEN POPPYSEED CASSEROLE

When the chicken is done cooking in the Instant Pot, let the pressure vent release naturally for 5 minutes, then manually release the remaining steam. For either cooking method, transfer the cooked chicken to a cutting board. When it's cool enough to handle, cut the chicken into bite-sized cubes and set aside.

Step 5:

SMOKY ROPA VIEJA WITH FRIED PLANTAINS

2 lbs (907 g) flank steak

Salt and pepper

2 tbsp (30 ml) olive oil (if using the stove)

2 (9-oz [255-g]) jars Mesa de Vida Smoky Latin Sauce

¼ cup (45 g) drained capers

After cutting the chicken, season the flank steak with salt and pepper and cut it into pieces that will fit inside an Instant Pot. Set your Instant Pot to the sauté setting and brown the flank steak on both sides, working in batches. Turn off the sauté setting and add the Smoky Latin Sauce and the capers to the meat in the Instant Pot. Seal and set to the Meat/Stew setting for 90 minutes.

If you do not have an Instant Pot, season your meat with salt and pepper. Heat the olive oil in a large Dutch oven or stew pot over medium-high heat. Add the beef and brown it on all sides, 3 to 4 minutes per side. When the steak is browned, remove it from the pot and add ½ cup (120 ml) of the Smoky Latin Sauce to the pot and scrape the bottom to release any brown bits. Return the steak to the pot, then add the remaining sauce and the capers. Bring to a boil, then reduce the heat to low, cover and simmer for 2 to 3 hours, until the steak is pull-apart tender.

Step 6:

GREEK CHICKEN TACOS WITH FETA SLAW

2 lbs (907 g) boneless, skinless chicken breasts

1 cup (240 ml) Paleo-friendly Greek dressing, divided

While the ropa vieja is cooking, divide the chicken breasts into two equal portions. Place each portion in an airtight resealable bag and pour ½ cup (120 ml) of Greek dressing into each bag. Squeeze the air out of the marinating bags and seal. Place one bag in the refrigerator for cook night and the other bag in the freezer for reheat night.

Step 7:

VIBRANT ROASTED ROOT VEGGIE BOWLS

After marinating the Greek chicken, remove the roasted vegetables from the oven and allow them to cool completely. Turn the oven down to 375°F (191°C). Divide the roasted vegetables into two equal portions. Add both portions into airtight containers and place one portion in the refrigerator for cook night and the other portion in the freezer for reheat night.

Step 8:

SMOKY ROPA VIEJA WITH FRIED PLANTAINS

Once the ropa vieja is done cooking, if you used the Instant Pot to cook it, let the steam release naturally for 10 to 15 minutes.

Once the ropa vieja is completely cooled, divide it into two equal portions and place them into airtight containers. Keep one portion in the refrigerator for cook night and the other portion in the freezer for reheat night.

THAI BASIL BEEF OVER COCONUT CAULIFLOWER RICE

2 lbs (907 g) flank steak

1 tbsp (15 ml) water

1 tbsp (8 g) arrowroot

1 tbsp (15 ml) coconut aminos

While the ropa vieja is naturally venting, slice the flank steak into ½-inch (1.3-cm) strips and then combine with the water, arrowroot and coconut aminos. Stir to coat the steak and set aside to marinate.

CHICKEN POPPYSEED CASSEROLE

4 cups (360 g) frozen hash browns

½ cup (64 g) arrowroot

4 cups (960 ml) chicken bone broth, divided

1 tbsp (18 g) salt

2 tbsp (18 g) gelatin

¾ cup (180 ml) coconut cream

2 tbsp (18 g) poppy seeds

TOPPING

1 cup (56 g) Paleo-friendly bread crumbs

2 cups (216 g) sliced almonds

1 tsp salt

While the Thai basil beef is marinating, preheat the oven to 350°F (177°C). Grease two 8 x 8-inch (20 x 20-cm) baking dishes, and arrange 2 cups (180 g) of hash browns at the bottom of each dish. Bake for 25 minutes.

While the hash browns are baking, make the "cream of chicken" soup. In a large soup pot over high heat, whisk the arrowroot and 2 cups (480 ml) of chicken bone broth together until no lumps remain. Add the remaining 2 cups (480 ml) of chicken broth and the salt and continue stirring constantly until the mixture comes to a boil. Add the gelatin and whisk until combined.

Add the coconut cream and poppy seeds and continue to whisk until combined. Add the chicken from step 2 to this mixture and stir to incorporate. Remove the pot from the heat.

Once the hash browns are done, divide the chicken mixture between the two baking dishes, pouring it on top of the hash browns.

In a small bowl, mix together the bread crumbs, almonds and salt. Divide the mixture in half and spread it evenly on top of both casserole dishes.

Bake both casseroles for 30 to 40 minutes, until golden and bubbly on top. After 20 minutes, rotate each baking dish and swap which racks they are on to ensure even cooking.

Step 11:

THAI BASIL BEEF OVER COCONUT
CAULIFLOWER RICE

2 tbsp (30 ml) olive oil

Salt and pepper

1 yellow onion, thinly sliced

2 medium carrots, julienned or coarsely grated

1 red bell pepper, julienned

5 cloves garlic, thinly sliced

1 (7-oz [198-g]) package Thai coconut sauce

While the Chicken Poppyseed Casseroles are baking, in a large skillet or wok, heat the olive oil over high heat. Season the marinated flank steak with salt and pepper and sear the beef, 2 to 3 minutes each side. Remove the beef from the pan and set aside. Add the sliced onion and julienned carrots to the same pan and cook for 5 minutes, until the vegetables are tender. Add the red bell pepper and the garlic and cook for 1 minute more. Add the coconut sauce and stir to combine.

Return the beef to the pan and cook over medium heat until the beef is completely cooked through and the sauce has thickened, 5 to 7 minutes. Let the mixture cool, then add both portions to airtight containers, and place one portion in the refrigerator for cook night and the other portion in the freezer for reheat night.

Step 12:

CHICKEN POPPYSEED CASSEROLE

Once the casseroles are done baking, remove them from the oven and allow both to completely cool. Cover both of the casseroles tightly with plastic wrap, then also wrap them in aluminum foil. Put one in the refrigerator for cook night and one in the freezer for reheat night.

GREEK CHICKEN TACOS WITH FETA SLAW

Serves 4 on cook night and 4 on reheat night with the additional fresh ingredients found in the reheat grocery list on page 153

Truly, I could put absolutely anything into a taco, and you will love these Greek chicken ones. Just when you thought we were done creating tortillas out of vegetables . . . I have found another way! Surprisingly, when eggplants are thinly sliced and roasted, they make a great tortilla. If you're feeling ambitious, they're a fun option—find the recipe on page 235! Otherwise, grain-free tortillas get the job done here.

½ recipe marinated chicken from the weekly prep (page 139)

SLAW
1 (10-oz [283-g]) bag coleslaw

2 scallions, thinly sliced

1 (6-oz [170-g]) package Paleo-friendly feta

½ tsp salt

½ tsp black pepper

½ cup (120 ml) Paleo-friendly Greek dressing

GARNISH
1 red onion, thinly sliced

1 cucumber, thinly sliced

1 pint (510 g) cherry tomatoes

3 tbsp (45 ml) Paleo-friendly Greek dressing

1 (8-piece) frozen package taco-sized grain-free tortillas

NOTE: If you'd prefer to make these elements from scratch, see page 231 for the Greek Dressing recipe and page 235 for the Eggplant Tortillas recipe.

PREP DAY:

See page 139 for the prep ingredients and instructions.

COOK NIGHT:

Remove the marinated chicken from the refrigerator.

Make the slaw by combining all the ingredients in a large bowl and tossing to combine. Set aside.

Heat a grill or grill pan on the stove over medium-high heat. Remove the chicken from the marinade and place on the hot grill. Grill the chicken for 5 to 6 minutes, then flip over to the other side and grill for an additional 5 to 6 minutes (or until cooked through and the internal temperature is 165°F [74°C] on an instant-read thermometer). Remove the chicken from the grill pan and let it rest.

While the chicken is resting, put the red onion, cucumber and tomatoes into a bowl and toss with the Greek dressing.

Slice the chicken breasts into thin slices on the diagonal.

Assemble your tacos by placing slices of chicken onto the tortillas and topping with the onion, cucumber and tomato mix. Serve with the slaw on the side.

REHEAT NIGHT:

To thaw the chicken overnight, move the container from the freezer to the refrigerator the night before reheat night. To thaw day of, move the container from the freezer to your countertop and allow the chicken to completely thaw at room temperature. For a quick thaw, submerge the container in room temperature water until completely thawed. Once thawed, follow the instructions for cook night.

VIBRANT ROASTED ROOT VEGGIE BOWLS

Serves 4 on cook night and 4 on reheat night with the additional fresh ingredients found in the reheat grocery list on page 153

My friend Myra, who is vegan, adores this recipe so much that she had a dream about it! The combination of root vegetables and tangy honey mustard keeps us making this recipe on repeat in our house. The homemade version of the dressing (on page 235) calls for grainy mustard, which is mustard that has whole grain mustard seeds in it. If you can't find it, feel free to double the Dijon.

½ recipe roasted vegetables from the weekly prep (page 138)

1 tbsp (15 ml) olive oil

1½ cups (219 g) raw cashews

1 (8-oz [237-ml]) jar Paleo-friendly honey mustard dressing

2 tbsp (30 ml) lemon juice

1 bunch parsley, leaves roughly chopped

PREP DAY:

See page 138 for the prep ingredients and instructions.

COOK NIGHT:

Remove the roasted vegetables from the refrigerator.

Heat the olive oil in a large cast-iron or regular skillet. Add the roasted vegetables and the raw cashews and sauté on medium-low heat until heated through, 5 to 7 minutes. Once the vegetables are warm, remove them from the heat and put them in a large bowl. Combine the honey mustard dressing with the lemon juice and parsley. Pour the dressing over them and toss to coat before serving.

REHEAT NIGHT:

To thaw the roasted vegetables overnight, move them from the freezer to the refrigerator the night before reheat night. To thaw day of, move the container from the freezer to your countertop and allow the roasted vegetables to completely thaw at room temperature. For a quick thaw, submerge the container in room temperature water until completely thawed. Once thawed, follow the instructions from cook night.

NOTE: If you'd prefer to make the dressing from scratch, see page 235 for the Honey Mustard Dressing recipe.

SMOKY ROPA VIEJA WITH FRIED PLANTAINS

Serves 4 on cook night and 4 on reheat night with the additional fresh ingredients found in the reheat grocery list on page 153

This recipe is such a crowd-pleaser. Ropa vieja is the national dish of Cuba, and it literally translates to "old clothes." The story goes that a man didn't have enough money for food, so he cooked his clothes. Miraculously, this dish was somehow born. Miracles aside, this beef-and-pepper dish is to die for!

½ recipe ropa vieja from the weekly prep (page 139)

4 tbsp (60 g) coconut oil

2 ripe plantains

Salt, to taste

Olives with pimientos, for garnish (optional)

PREP DAY:

See page 139 for the prep ingredients and instructions.

COOK NIGHT:

Remove the ropa vieja from the refrigerator and pour it into a large pot on the stovetop. Heat it over medium heat until it's heated through, stirring occasionally, 8 to 10 minutes.

While the ropa vieja is reheating, heat the coconut oil in a large skillet over medium heat. Peel and slice the plantains on a diagonal and, working in batches, fry them until golden brown and tender, about 3 minutes each side. Remove them from the pan and lightly sprinkle them with salt.

Serve the ropa vieja with the fried plantains and garnished with the olives, if desired.

REHEAT NIGHT:

To thaw the ropa vieja overnight, move it from the freezer to the refrigerator the night before reheat night. To thaw day of, move the container from the freezer to your countertop and allow it to completely thaw at room temperature. For a quick thaw, submerge the container in room temperature water until completely thawed. Once thawed, follow the cook night instructions.

NOTE: If you'd prefer to make the sauce for the ropa vieja from scratch, see page 236 for the full recipe.

CHICKEN POPPYSEED CASSEROLE

Serves 4 on cook night and 4 on reheat night

Chicken Poppyseed Casserole is a Southern classic. I make it for all of my friends in Colorado because it's a darn *shame* that they've never had it! It's creamy comfort food at its finest. It's traditionally full of cream of this and cream of that, so I cleaned up the ingredients and made it Paleo for you. Since you put in all the hard work on prep day, all you have to do is reheat it night of! That means this casserole goes from fridge to plate in less than an hour with zero hands-on time.

1 casserole from the weekly prep (pages 138 and 140)

PREP DAY:

See pages 138 and 140 for the prep ingredients and instructions.

COOK NIGHT:

Remove the casserole from the refrigerator and let it stand at room temperature for 30 minutes while preheating the oven to 350°F (177°C).

Remove the aluminum foil and the plastic wrap from the baking dish and replace the aluminum foil. Reheat it in the oven until completely warmed through, 25 to 30 minutes. Slice the casserole into four portions and serve.

REHEAT NIGHT:

To thaw the casserole, remove it from the freezer to the refrigerator the night before reheat night. Once the casserole has thawed, follow the instructions for cook night.

THAI BASIL BEEF OVER COCONUT CAULIFLOWER RICE

Serves 4 on cook night and 4 on reheat night with the additional fresh ingredients found in the reheat grocery list on page 153

This is one of the most popular Thai dishes, which is no surprise to me because I order it at Thai restaurants all the time! There are many variations of Thai dishes similar to this one with meat and seafood stir-fried with basil on top. This beef version is paired with a dark, rich and flavorful sauce you will love. You can also top this dish with a fried egg if you're feeling ambitious! Holy basil leaves truly make this dish, but you can use Thai basil or fresh Italian basil leaves, if desired.

½ recipe Thai basil beef mixture from the weekly prep (page 140)

3 cups (72 g) fresh holy basil, chopped, divided

1 bunch cilantro, for garnish (optional)

1 lime, cut into wedges (for serving)

COCONUT CAULIFLOWER RICE

1 tsp coconut oil

4 cups (453 g) frozen cauli-flower rice

1 cup (240 ml) coconut milk

Zest of 1 lime

¼ cup (4 g) cilantro, roughly chopped

PREP DAY:

See pages 140 and 141 for the prep ingredients and instructions.

COOK NIGHT:

Pour the Thai basil beef mixture from the refrigerator into a large skillet or wok over medium heat. After it is warmed through, about 5 minutes, add 1½ cups (36 g) of the basil and stir to wilt.

While that's heating, make the coconut cauliflower rice. Heat the coconut oil in a large skillet. Add the cauliflower rice and coconut milk and cook for 5 to 8 minutes, until it is warmed and the liquid has cooked off.

Remove the cauliflower rice from the heat and stir in the lime zest and cilantro.

Serve the Thai basil beef over the coconut cauliflower rice and garnish with cilantro, if desired, the other half of the fresh holy basil and a lime wedge.

REHEAT NIGHT:

To thaw the Thai basil beef overnight, move it from the freezer to the refrigerator the night before reheat night. To thaw day of, move the container from the freezer to your countertop and allow it to completely thaw at room temperature. For a quick thaw, submerge each container in room temperature water until completely thawed. Once thawed, follow the instructions for cook night.

NOTE: If you prefer to make the Thai basil sauce entirely from scratch, see page 236 for the recipe.

WEEK 8 GROCERY LIST

PROTEIN

- ☐ 4 lbs (1.8 kg) boneless, skinless chicken breasts ● ●
- ☐ 4 lbs (1.8 kg) flank steak ● ●

PRODUCE

- ☐ 1 bunch parsley ●
- ☐ 1 (10-oz [283-g]) bag coleslaw ●
- ☐ 1 bunch scallions ●
- ☐ 1 red onion ●
- ☐ 1 cucumber ●
- ☐ 1 pint (510 g) cherry tomatoes ●
- ☐ 2 heads cauliflower ●
- ☐ 4 sweet potatoes ●
- ☐ 1 lemon ●
- ☐ 2 large golden beets ●
- ☐ 1 yellow onion ●
- ☐ 2 red bell peppers ●
- ☐ 1 head garlic ● ●
- ☐ 2 ripe plantains ●
- ☐ 2 carrots ●
- ☐ 2 limes ●
- ☐ 1 bunch cilantro ●
- ☐ 3 cups (72 g) holy basil ●

PANTRY

- ☐ ¼ cup (45 g) capers ●
- ☐ Coconut oil ● ●
- ☐ 1½ cups (219 g) raw cashews ●
- ☐ 1 (7- to 10-oz [198- to 283-g]) jar olives with pimientos ●
- ☐ 2 (32-oz [960-ml]) boxes chicken bone broth ●
- ☐ Arrowroot ● ●
- ☐ 1 (13.5-oz [398-ml]) jar coconut cream ●
- ☐ 2 tbsp (18 g) gelatin ●
- ☐ 2 cups (216 g) sliced almonds ●
- ☐ Coconut aminos ●

- ☐ 1 (13.5-oz [398-ml]) can coconut milk ●
- ☐ 1 (8-oz [237-ml]) jar Paleo-friendly honey mustard dressing (I like Primal Kitchen Honey Mustard Dressing & Marinade) ●
- ☐ 2 (8-oz [236-ml]) jars Paleo-friendly Greek dressing (I like Primal Kitchen Greek Vinaigrette & Marinade) ●
- ☐ 2 (9-oz [255-g]) jars Paleo-friendly Latin sauce (I like Mesa de Vida Smoky Latin Sauce) ●
- ☐ 1 (7-oz [198-g]) package Thai coconut sauce (I like Kevin's Thai Coconut Sauce) ●
- ☐ 1 cup (56 g) Paleo-friendly bread crumbs (I like Jeff Nathan Creations Chef Gourmet Panko Plain Gluten Free) ●

FREEZER

- ☐ 4 cups (360 g) frozen hash browns ●
- ☐ 4 cups (453 g) frozen cauliflower rice ●
- ☐ 1 (8-piece) frozen package taco-sized grain-free tortillas ●

SPICES

- ☐ Poppy seeds ●

DAIRY ALTERNATIVES

- ☐ 1 (6-oz [170-g]) package Paleo-friendly feta (I like Violife vegan feta) ●

RECIPES KEY: ● ● ● ● ●

| Greek Chicken Tacos with Feta Slaw (page 142) |
| Smoky Ropa Vieja with Fried Plantains (page 146) |
| Chicken Poppyseed Casserole (page 149) |
| Vibrant Roasted Root Veggie Bowls (page 145) |
| Thai Basil Beef over Coconut Cauliflower Rice (page 150) |

WEEK 8 REHEAT GROCERY LIST

GREEK CHICKEN TACOS WITH FETA SLAW

- ☐ 1 (10-oz [283-g]) bag coleslaw
- ☐ 1 bunch scallions
- ☐ 1 (6-oz [170-g]) package Paleo-friendly feta (I like Violife vegan feta)
- ☐ 1 red onion
- ☐ 1 cucumber
- ☐ 1 pint (510 g) cherry tomatoes
- ☐ 1 (8-oz [236-ml]) jar Paleo-friendly Greek dressing (I like Primal Kitchen Greek Vinaigrette & Marinade)
- ☐ 1 (8-piece) frozen package taco-sized grain-free tortillas

VIBRANT ROASTED ROOT VEGGIE BOWLS

- ☐ 1 (8-oz [237-ml]) jar Paleo-friendly honey mustard dressing (I like Primal Kitchen Honey Mustard Dressing & Marinade)
- ☐ 1½ cups (219 g) raw cashews

SMOKY ROPA VIEJA WITH FRIED PLANTAINS

- ☐ 2 ripe plantains
- ☐ Coconut oil
- ☐ 1 (7- to 10-oz [198- to 283-g]) jar olives with pimientos

CHICKEN POPPYSEED CASSEROLE

- ☐ Nothing needed

THAI BASIL BEEF OVER COCONUT CAULIFLOWER RICE

- ☐ Coconut oil
- ☐ 4 cups (453 g) frozen cauliflower rice
- ☐ 1 (13.5-oz [398-ml]) can coconut milk
- ☐ 2 limes
- ☐ 1 bunch cilantro, for garnish (optional)
- ☐ 3 cups (72 g) holy basil

WEEK 9

The beef stew that kicks off this week perfectly fuses Caribbean flavors with a classic American favorite, and the mashed plantains it's served with are packed with flavor. I hope I get to introduce you to North Carolina barbecue sauce with the Tangy Carolina Vinegar Barbecue. I don't want to exaggerate, but the pork nachos are going to change your life. Meanwhile, the Umami Mushroom Lettuce Wraps are so quick to bring together and will transport you to your favorite Asian restaurant. And the Rustic Hungarian Goulash recipe is a set-it-and-forget-it recipe you'll make on repeat!

WEEK 9 PREP-DAY INSTRUCTIONS

This is yet another week where you get to speed up prep day by cooking the pork once for two separate recipes. If you don't use beef stew meat often, you will now! Since it's conveniently already cut when you buy it, you can literally just throw it in a dish. It drastically reduces hands-on time and is fall-apart tender. You'll cook the Caribbean beef stew in a Dutch oven on the stovetop while the pork cooks in your Instant Pot (or on the stovetop). The filling for the lettuce wraps comes together in minutes, and the Rustic Hungarian Goulash is so fuss-free, you'll forget it's cooking away while you prep.

Step 1:

PULLED PORK FOR TANGY CAROLINA VINEGAR BARBECUE & UNBELIEVABLE PULLED PORK NACHOS

4 lbs (1.8 kg) pork butt roast, boneless

4 tbsp (30 g) Primal Palate Organic Spices Barbecue Rub

2 tbsp (30 ml) olive oil

4 cups (960 ml) chicken bone broth, divided

1 tbsp (15 ml) coconut aminos

1 bay leaf

To make the pulled pork, trim the excess fat from the pork and cut it into four even pieces.

In a large bowl, combine the pork and spice rub and toss to coat.

Set your Instant Pot to the sauté setting and add the olive oil, or skip ahead for the stovetop instructions. Working in batches, brown all sides of each piece of pork, 3 to 4 minutes per side.

Once all the pieces of pork are seared, set them aside. Turn off the Instant Pot and add ½ cup (120 ml) of the chicken bone broth, scraping the bottom of the pot to loosen the brown bits.

Add the remaining chicken bone broth, the coconut aminos and bay leaf.

Return the pork to the Instant Pot. Secure the lid and check that the vent is set to seal. Cook on High Pressure for 60 minutes. Let the pressure release naturally.

If you do not have an Instant Pot, preheat the oven to 300°F (149°C). Heat the olive oil in a large Dutch oven. Working in batches, brown all sides of each piece of pork, 3 to 4 minutes per side. Once all the pork is seared, remove it from the pot and set it aside. Add ½ cup (120 ml) of the bone broth and scrape the brown bits from the bottom of the pot. Return the pork to the pot and add the remaining chicken bone broth, the coconut aminos and bay leaf. Cover the pot and place it in the oven for 2 to 3 hours. Check the internal temperature of the pork using an instant-read thermometer. When it reaches 180 to 190°F (82 to 88°C) remove it from the oven (this is a higher temperature than normal, but it is necessary to break down the collagen and give you that pull-apart tenderness).

Step 2:

CARIBBEAN BEEF STEW WITH MASHED PLANTAINS

2 tbsp (30 ml) olive oil

2 lbs (907 g) beef stew meat, cut into 1-inch (2.5-cm) cubes

Salt and pepper

1 yellow onion, diced

2 cloves garlic, thinly sliced

1 (1-inch [2.5-cm]) piece fresh ginger, minced

1 tsp ground cinnamon

1 tbsp (2 g) fresh thyme leaves, chopped

1 Scotch bonnet pepper, stemmed, seeded and minced (optional)

4 cups (960 ml) beef bone broth

While the pulled pork is cooking, start on the Caribbean beef stew. In a large Dutch oven, heat the olive oil over medium heat. Season the stew meat with salt and pepper, then add it to the pot and cook until browned on all sides, 5 to 7 minutes.

Remove the beef from the Dutch oven and set aside. Add the onion and sauté until translucent, about 5 minutes. Add the garlic, ginger, cinnamon, thyme and Scotch bonnet pepper (if using) and sauté until fragrant, about 2 minutes more.

Return the beef to the pot and add the beef bone broth. Bring to a boil, then lower to a simmer. Cover and simmer for 45 minutes.

Step 3:

UMAMI MUSHROOM LETTUCE WRAPS

2 tbsp (30 ml) olive oil

2 shallots, finely diced

2 lbs (907 g) mixed mushrooms (any mixture of baby bella, crimini, shiitake, maitake), roughly chopped

2 cloves garlic, minced

1 tbsp (9 g) freshly grated ginger

Pinch of red pepper flakes

While the Caribbean beef stew is simmering, you'll work on the filling for the Umami Mushroom Lettuce Wraps. Heat the olive oil in a large sauté pan or Dutch oven over medium heat. Add the shallots and cook until translucent, about 2 minutes. Add the mushrooms and sauté until they've cooked down and are beginning to brown, 5 to 7 minutes. Add the garlic, ginger and red pepper flakes. Sauté until fragrant, about 1 minute more.

⅓ cup (80 ml) coconut aminos

1 tbsp (15 ml) rice wine vinegar

1 tbsp (15 ml) honey

1 tbsp (15 ml) Paleo-friendly sriracha

While the mushrooms are cooking, in a small bowl, whisk together the coconut aminos, rice wine vinegar, honey and sriracha. Set aside.

(continued)

1 (8-oz [226-g]) can whole water chestnuts, drained and diced

3 scallions, thinly sliced

1 cup (146 g) raw cashews, roughly chopped

Salt and pepper, to taste

Add the water chestnuts, scallions and cashews to the mushrooms and sauté until the scallions are tender, 3 to 5 minutes. Season to taste with salt and pepper.

Remove the pan from the heat, stir in the sauce and allow it to completely cool.

Divide the sautéed mushrooms into two equal portions. Place each portion in an airtight container or resealable bag. Place one container in the refrigerator for cook night and the other portion in the freezer for reheat night.

Step 4:

CARIBBEAN BEEF STEW WITH MASHED PLANTAINS

1 (13.5-oz [398-ml]) can coconut milk

2 large sweet potatoes, peeled and cut into ½-inch (1.3-cm) dice

Once the Caribbean stew has cooked for 45 minutes, add the coconut milk and diced sweet potatoes, cover and simmer for an additional 15 to 20 minutes, until the sweet potatoes are tender.

Remove the stew from the heat and allow it to cool completely. Divide the stew into two equal portions. Place each portion in an airtight container. Store one portion in the refrigerator for cook night and the other portion in the freezer for reheat night.

Step 5:

UNBELIEVABLE PULLED PORK NACHOS & TANGY CAROLINA VINEGAR BARBECUE WITH BROCCOLI SLAW

While the Caribbean beef stew is cooking, transfer the pork to a cutting board and shred it using two forks.

Divide the pork into two equal portions (one portion for the nachos and one portion for the barbecue). Then take each portion and divide that in half, keeping 2 quarters in the refrigerator for each cook night and the other 2 quarters in the freezer for reheat night. Be sure to properly label each portion.

RUSTIC HUNGARIAN GOULASH

2 tbsp (30 ml) olive oil

2 yellow onions, diced

4 carrots, cut in ¼-inch (6-mm) rounds and then fourths

1 red bell pepper, chopped

1 yellow bell pepper, chopped

2 cloves garlic, minced

2 tsp (12 g) salt

1 tsp black pepper

2 tbsp (14 g) Hungarian paprika

1 tsp caraway seeds

¼ cup (32 g) arrowroot

4 russet potatoes, large dice

1 (15-oz [425-g]) can diced tomatoes

2 lbs (907 g) beef stew meat

4 cups (960 ml) beef bone broth

After storing the pulled pork, set your Instant Pot setting to sauté and when hot, add the olive oil (or skip ahead for the stovetop instructions). Add the onions, carrots and red and yellow bell peppers. Sauté for 5 minutes until the vegetables are tender. Add the garlic and sauté while stirring, 1 minute more.

Add the salt, pepper, Hungarian paprika, caraway seeds and arrowroot and stir to coat the vegetables. Turn off the Instant Pot.

Add the potatoes, diced tomatoes, stew meat and beef bone broth and stir to combine.

Place the lid on the Instant Pot and seal the vent. Click the Meat/Stew setting and set it to 60 minutes.

After this is finished, allow the vent to naturally release for 15 minutes, then manually release any remaining pressure. Turn off the Instant Pot, remove the goulash and allow it to cool completely.

If you do not have an Instant Pot, season the stew meat with salt and pepper and set aside. In a large Dutch oven or stew pot, heat the olive oil over medium heat. Add the stew meat and cook until browned on all sides. Add the chopped onions and sauté until translucent, about 5 minutes. Add the garlic and sauté until fragrant, about 1 more minute. Add the paprika and caraway seeds and sauté until fragrant, 1 additional minute. Add the arrowroot and stir until all ingredients are coated. Add the bone broth, diced tomatoes, bell peppers, carrots and potatoes, then stir to combine. Bring to a boil, then reduce to a simmer, cover and cook on low for 1½ to 2 hours, until the meat is tender.

Divide the goulash into two equal portions and store each portion in an airtight container. Place one portion in the refrigerator for cook night and the other portion in the freezer for reheat night.

CARIBBEAN BEEF STEW WITH MASHED PLANTAINS

Serves 4 on cook night and 4 on reheat night with the additional fresh ingredients found in the reheat grocery list on page 171

When making these mashed plantains, I said, "*Why* haven't I ever thought of this before?!" I'm a huge fan of plantains, and this just gives me an extra way to enjoy them. The spices go well with this Caribbean take on beef stew, which includes garlic, cinnamon and sweet potatoes. I especially love this recipe in the fall and winter, as it makes your home smell fantastic as it's cooking!

½ recipe beef stew from the weekly prep (page 157)

Salt and pepper, to taste

Scallions, chopped, for garnish (optional)

MASHED PLANTAINS

4 ripe plantains

2 tbsp (30 g) coconut oil

1 (13.5-oz [398-ml]) can coconut milk

1 tsp salt

½ tsp black pepper

¼ tsp cinnamon

1½ tbsp (21 g) unsalted ghee

PREP DAY:

See page 157 for the prep ingredients and instructions.

COOK NIGHT:

Remove the stew from the refrigerator and pour it into a soup pot or Dutch oven on the stovetop. Reheat the stew over medium heat until heated through, 8 to 10 minutes.

While the stew is reheating, make the mashed plantains. Peel the plantains and slice into 1-inch (2.5-cm) pieces. In a large Dutch oven, melt the coconut oil. Add the plantains to the pot and stir to coat them in the oil. Sauté them for 2 minutes to start to soften them. Add the coconut milk and salt and bring to a gentle simmer. Simmer, uncovered, for 10 minutes, until the plantains are fork-tender. Remove them from the heat and add them (with the coconut milk) to a stand mixer fitted with the paddle attachment. Add the pepper, cinnamon and ghee and mix until well combined and the plantains are your desired consistency.

Once the stew is hot, remove it from the heat and season to taste with salt and pepper. Garnish it with the chopped scallions, if using, and serve over the mashed plantains.

REHEAT NIGHT:

To thaw the stew overnight, move it from the freezer to the refrigerator the night before reheat night. To thaw day of, move the container from the freezer to your countertop and allow the stew to completely thaw at room temperature. For a quick thaw, submerge the container in room temperature water until completely thawed. Once thawed, follow the instructions for cook night.

UMAMI MUSHROOM LETTUCE WRAPS

Serves 4 on cook night and 4 on reheat night with the additional fresh ingredients found in the reheat grocery list on page 171

Growing up, we would always get lettuce wraps when we went to Asian restaurants, and it was my favorite part of the entire meal! These Umami Mushroom Lettuce Wraps are vegetarian, featuring a mix of mushrooms. Even though this is a meatless meal, the mushrooms and cashews make it hearty. I love vegetarian meals like this that are so fast to whip together!

½ recipe mushroom filling from the weekly prep (page 157)

2 heads butter lettuce

6 scallions, sliced, for serving (optional)

PREP DAY:

See page 157 for the prep ingredients and instructions.

COOK NIGHT:

Remove the cooked mushrooms from the refrigerator and pour them into a large sauté pan or Dutch oven. Reheat them on the stovetop over medium heat until warmed through, about 5 minutes.

While the mushrooms are reheating, wash and dry the butter lettuce leaves and set them aside.

To serve, add a large spoonful of mushrooms to each lettuce leaf and garnish with sliced scallions, if desired.

REHEAT NIGHT:

To thaw the mushrooms overnight, move them from the freezer to the refrigerator the night before reheat night. To thaw day of, move the container from the freezer to your countertop and allow the mushrooms to completely thaw at room temperature. For a quick thaw, submerge the container in room temperature water until completely thawed. Once thawed, follow the instructions for cook night.

TANGY CAROLINA VINEGAR BARBECUE WITH BROCCOLI SLAW

Serves 4 on cook night and 4 on reheat night with the additional fresh ingredients found in the reheat grocery list on page 171

I have such a deep appreciation for every single variation of barbecue. Barbecue sauces vary greatly across the country, and if you've never had a vinegar-style barbecue sauce, you are in for a treat! Originating in North Carolina, this barbecue sauce is both tangy and spicy. It's a nice, light sauce that truly brings out the flavors of your pulled pork.

BROCCOLI SLAW

½ cup (120 ml) Paleo-friendly mayonnaise

2 tbsp (30 ml) honey

1 tsp Dijon mustard

1 tbsp (9 g) poppy seeds

1 (12-oz [340-g]) bag broccoli slaw

¼ cup (34 g) sunflower seeds

1 Pink Lady apple, diced

¼ cup (40 g) red onion, ¼-inch (6-mm) dice

BARBECUE PORK

1 lb (454 g) shredded pork from the weekly prep (page 156)

1 (12-oz [340-g]) jar Paleo-friendly barbecue sauce

Paleo buns, store-bought or homemade (page 226), or 4 leaves Bibb lettuce for lettuce cups

PREP DAY:

See page 156 for the instructions to prep this recipe.

COOK NIGHT:

In a small bowl, add the mayonnaise, honey, mustard and poppy seeds. Whisk together until well combined. In a large serving bowl, toss together the broccoli slaw, sunflower seeds, diced apple and red onion. Pour the dressing into the slaw and toss to coat.

Combine the pulled pork and barbecue sauce in a skillet and reheat the pork over medium heat until heated through, 7 to 10 minutes. Serve the barbecue pork on Paleo buns or lettuce cups with the slaw.

REHEAT NIGHT:

To thaw the pulled pork overnight, move it from the freezer to the refrigerator the night before reheat night. To thaw day of, move the container from the freezer to your countertop and allow the pork to completely thaw at room temperature. For a quick thaw, submerge the container in room temperature water until completely thawed. Once thawed, follow the instructions for cook night.

NOTE: If you'd prefer to make the sauce, buns and spice rub from scratch, see page 237 for the Carolina Vinegar Sauce recipe, page 226 for the Paleo Buns recipe and page 229 for the Spice Rub recipe.

RUSTIC HUNGARIAN GOULASH

Serves 4 on cook night and 4 on reheat night with the additional fresh ingredients found in the reheat grocery list on page 171

Goulash is a hearty meat-and-vegetable soup that is seasoned with paprika. It originated in Hungary and is one of the country's national dishes. There are many different varieties of Hungarian goulash, but ours uses garlic, bell peppers, carrots, potatoes and tomatoes. Using pre-cut stew meat is a great way to make a meal even faster, and when cooked it is cut-with-a-fork tender.

½ recipe goulash from the weekly prep (page 159)

1 (9-oz [255-g]) box Paleo-friendly noodles

¾ cup (180 ml) unsweetened plain Paleo-friendly yogurt, for serving (optional)

PREP DAY:

See page 159 for the prep ingredients and instructions.

COOK NIGHT:

Remove the goulash from the refrigerator and pour it into a soup pot or Dutch oven. Reheat the goulash over medium heat until heated through, 8 to 10 minutes.

Meanwhile, bring a large pot of salted water to a boil on the stovetop. Cook the Paleo noodles according to package directions. Drain the noodles and serve with the goulash and a dollop of yogurt, if using.

REHEAT NIGHT:

To thaw the goulash overnight, move it from the freezer to the refrigerator the night before reheat night. To thaw day of, move the container from the freezer to your countertop and allow the goulash to completely thaw at room temperature. For a quick thaw, submerge the container in room temperature water until completely thawed. Once thawed, follow the instructions for cook night.

UNBELIEVABLE PULLED PORK NACHOS

Serves 4 on cook night and 4 on reheat night with the additional fresh ingredients found in the reheat grocery list on page 171

Mmmm . . . nachos! I shared this recipe with a friend of mine and *all four* of their kiddos said this is their new all-time favorite meal—what an honor! This recipe is the ultimate weekend food, but made cleaner. I make these for football games (go dawgs!) or when hosting friends. This is the ultimate crowd-pleaser and a really fun weeknight meal.

2 cups (450 g) pulled pork from the weekly prep (page 156)

2 (5-oz [142-g]) bags grain-free tortilla chips

1 (10.8-oz [306-g]) jar Paleo-friendly queso

½ cup (80 g) red onion, thinly sliced

2 Roma tomatoes, diced

1 bunch cilantro, for garnish

1 (16-oz [454-g]) container unsweetened plain Paleo-friendly yogurt

PREP DAY:

See page 156 for the instructions to prep this recipe.

COOK NIGHT:

Remove the pulled pork from the refrigerator and add it to a large skillet on the stovetop. Reheat the pork over medium heat until warmed through, 8 to 10 minutes. While the pork is reheating, line a large baking sheet with aluminum foil. Spread out a layer of tortilla chips. Assemble the nachos by adding the pork topped with the queso. Turn the broiler in your oven on high. Place the baking sheet in the oven and broil the nachos for 3 to 5 minutes, until the queso is melty and the chips are toasty.

Remove the nachos from the oven and top with sliced red onion, diced tomatoes, cilantro and plain yogurt (it tastes like sour cream!).

REHEAT NIGHT:

To thaw the pulled pork overnight, move it from the freezer to the refrigerator the night before reheat night. To thaw day of, move the container from the freezer to your countertop and allow the pork to completely thaw at room temperature. For a quick thaw, submerge the container in room temperature water until completely thawed. Once thawed, follow the cook night instructions to assemble the nachos.

NOTE: If you'd prefer to make the pulled pork using a homemade spice rub, see page 229 for the recipe.

WEEK 9 GROCERY LIST

PROTEIN
- ☐ 4 lbs (1.8 kg) beef stew meat ● ●
- ☐ 4 lbs (1.8 kg) boneless pork butt roast ● ●

PRODUCE
- ☐ 3 yellow onions ● ●
- ☐ 1 head garlic ● ● ●
- ☐ 1 (2-inch [5-cm]) piece fresh ginger ● ●
- ☐ 1 bunch thyme ●
- ☐ 1 Scotch bonnet pepper (optional) ●
- ☐ 2 large sweet potatoes ●
- ☐ 2 bunches scallions ● ●
- ☐ 4 ripe plantains ●
- ☐ 2 shallots ●
- ☐ 2 lbs (907 g) mushrooms (any mixture of baby bella, crimini, shiitake or maitake) ●
- ☐ 2 heads butter/Bibb lettuce ●
- ☐ 1 (12-oz [340-g]) bag broccoli slaw ●
- ☐ 1 Pink Lady apple ●
- ☐ 2 red onions ● ●
- ☐ 4 large carrots ●
- ☐ 1 red bell pepper ●
- ☐ 1 yellow bell pepper ●
- ☐ 4 russet potatoes ●
- ☐ 2 Roma tomatoes ●
- ☐ 1 bunch cilantro ●

SPICES
- ☐ Ground cinnamon ●
- ☐ Red pepper flakes ●
- ☐ Poppy seeds ●
- ☐ Hungarian paprika ●
- ☐ Caraway seeds ●
- ☐ Bay leaf ● ●
- ☐ Spice rub (I like Primal Palate Organic Spices Barbecue Rub) ● ●

PANTRY
- ☐ 2 (32-oz [960-ml]) boxes beef bone broth ● ●
- ☐ 2 (13.5-oz [398-ml]) cans coconut milk ●
- ☐ Coconut oil ●
- ☐ 7 tbsp (95 ml) coconut aminos ● ● ●
- ☐ Rice wine vinegar ●
- ☐ Honey ● ●
- ☐ Sriracha (I like Yellowbird Organic Sriracha) ●
- ☐ 1 cup (146 g) raw cashews ●
- ☐ 1 (8-oz [226-g]) can water chestnuts ●
- ☐ 1 (32-oz [960-ml]) box chicken bone broth ● ●
- ☐ ½ cup (120 ml) Paleo-friendly mayonnaise ●
- ☐ Dijon mustard ●
- ☐ ¼ cup (34 g) sunflower seeds ●
- ☐ Arrowroot ●
- ☐ 1 (15-oz [425-g]) can diced tomatoes ●
- ☐ 1 (9-oz [255-g]) box Paleo-friendly noodles (I like Cappello's Fettuccine Noodles) ●
- ☐ 2 (5-oz [142-g]) bags grain-free tortilla chips (I like Siete brand) ●
- ☐ 1 (10.8-oz [306-g]) jar Paleo-friendly queso (I like Siete brand) ●
- ☐ 1 (12-oz [340-g]) jar Paleo-friendly barbecue sauce (I like Noble Made Classic Marinade) ●

DAIRY ALTERNATIVES
- ☐ Unsalted ghee (I like Fourth & Heart) ●
- ☐ 2 (5.3-oz [150-g]) containers unsweetened plain Paleo-friendly yogurt (I like Forager Project Cashewmilk Yogurt) ● ●

FREEZER
- ☐ 1 package Paleo buns (if not making your own on page 226) ●

RECIPES KEY: ● ● ● ● ●

Caribbean Beef Stew with Mashed Plantains (page 160)
Tangy Carolina Vinegar Barbecue with Broccoli Slaw (page 164)
Rustic Hungarian Goulash (page 167)
Umami Mushroom Lettuce Wraps (page 163)
Unbelievable Pulled Pork Nachos (page 168)

CARIBBEAN BEEF STEW WITH MASHED PLANTAINS

- ☐ 1 bunch scallions, for garnish (optional)
- ☐ 4 ripe plantains
- ☐ Coconut oil
- ☐ 1 (13.5-oz [398-ml]) can coconut milk
- ☐ Unsalted ghee (I like Fourth & Heart)
- ☐ Cinnamon

UMAMI MUSHROOM LETTUCE WRAPS

- ☐ 2 heads butter/Bibb lettuce
- ☐ 1 bunch scallions

TANGY CAROLINA VINEGAR BARBECUE WITH BROCCOLI SLAW

- ☐ 1 (12-oz [340-g]) bag broccoli slaw
- ☐ ½ cup (120 ml) Paleo-friendly mayonnaise
- ☐ Honey
- ☐ Dijon mustard
- ☐ Poppy seeds
- ☐ 1 Pink Lady apple
- ☐ 1 red onion
- ☐ 1 (12-oz [340-g]) jar Paleo-friendly barbecue sauce (I like Noble Made Classic Marinade)
- ☐ ¼ cup (34 g) sunflower seeds
- ☐ 1 package Paleo buns (if not making your own on page 226)

RUSTIC HUNGARIAN GOULASH

- ☐ 1 (9-oz [255-g]) box Paleo-friendly noodles (I like Cappello's Fettuccine Noodles)
- ☐ 1 (5.3-oz [150-g]) container unsweetened plain Paleo-friendly yogurt (I like Forager Project Unsweetened Plain Cashewmilk Yogurt)

UNBELIEVABLE PULLED PORK NACHOS

- ☐ 2 (5-oz [142-g]) bags grain-free tortilla chips (I like Siete brand)
- ☐ 1 (10.8-oz [306-g]) jar Paleo-friendly queso (I like Siete brand)
- ☐ 1 red onion
- ☐ 2 Roma tomatoes
- ☐ 1 bunch cilantro
- ☐ 1 (5.3-oz [150-g]) container unsweetened plain Paleo yogurt (I like Forager Project Unsweetened Plain Cashewmilk Yogurt)

WEEK 10

Jamaican Jerk Chicken Bowls (page 178)

Saucy Scallion Meatballs with Asian Green Beans (page 181)

Hearty Minestrone with Gnocchi (page 182)

Harissa Chicken with Charred Lemons
and Crispy Potatoes (page 185)

Make-Ahead Enchilada Bake (page 186)

This week might be the book's most culturally diverse week, with flavors from the Caribbean, Italy, Asia, North Africa and Mexico. Week 10 features ground beef and chicken thighs, but if you're not a fan of chicken thighs, you can replace them with chicken breasts. The Make-Ahead Enchilada Bake is hands-down the recipe I've made the most since writing this cookbook. And you will be so glad to find the Paleo gnocchi for the minestrone. I use it as pasta with whatever sauce I have on hand for a superfast dinner!

WEEK 10 PREP-DAY INSTRUCTIONS

This week's jerk chicken and harissa chicken are both so full of unique flavors, and all you have to do today is marinate the chicken. I love that with the enchilada bake, you make two and freeze one so that you have a completely hands-off meal for a busy weeknight. The Hearty Minestrone with Gnocchi only requires some veggie chopping *and* is a healthy and flavorful vegetarian meal. The scallion meatballs are a breeze to make: You batch cook them in the oven for an easier approach to meatballs.

Step 1:

MAKE-AHEAD ENCHILADA BAKE

2 lbs (907 g) ground beef

1 tbsp (15 ml) olive oil

1 yellow onion, diced

3 cups (402 g) sweet potatoes, peeled and cut into ¼-inch (6-mm) dice

3 bell peppers (red, yellow or orange), cut into ¼-inch (6-mm) dice

To make the enchilada bake, first preheat your oven to 375°F (191°C).

Heat a large pot or Dutch oven over medium-high heat, add the beef and cook until it's browned and cooked through, 7 to 10 minutes.

Remove the beef from the pan and set it aside. Reduce the heat to medium and add the olive oil and diced onion, sweet potatoes and bell peppers. Sauté until the vegetables are tender and starting to brown, 10 to 15 minutes.

Step 2:

JAMAICAN JERK CHICKEN BOWLS

¼ cup (60 ml) olive oil

1 tbsp (15 ml) lime juice

1 jalapeño or Scotch bonnet pepper, seeded and finely chopped (optional)

2 to 3 tbsp (20 to 30 g) Paleo-friendly jerk seasoning

2 lbs (907 g) boneless, skinless chicken thighs

While the vegetables are sautéing, make the jerk marinade for the chicken. In a small bowl combine the olive oil, lime juice, chopped pepper (if using) and the jerk seasoning and whisk to combine.

Divide the chicken thighs into two equal portions and place each portion into its own resealable bag, pouring equal amounts of the marinade into each bag. Squeeze out the air and seal. Place one bag in the refrigerator for cook night (*Note: If it will be more than 2 days before you cook the chicken, place it in the freezer*). Place the other portion in the freezer for reheat night.

Step 3:

MAKE-AHEAD ENCHILADA BAKE

2 cloves garlic, minced

2 (8-piece) packages taco-sized grain-free tortillas

4½ cups (1.1 L) Paleo-friendly enchilada sauce

After you have finished the jerk chicken marinade, return to your enchilada vegetables. Once the vegetables are tender, still over medium heat, add the minced garlic and sauté until fragrant, about 1 more minute. Return the beef to the pot with the vegetables and stir to combine. Remove from the heat and set aside.

Start assembling the enchilada bake by spraying two 8 x 8-inch (20 x 20-cm) baking dishes with avocado oil cooking spray and set aside.

Add a layer of tortillas to the bottom of each pan. Place a full tortilla in the middle, then cut two tortillas in half, and place the flat edge of each on each flat side of the dish (so the round parts will all be facing the middle).

In each baking dish, add 2 cups of the beef-and-vegetable mixture, then ¾ cup (180 ml) enchilada sauce. Add another layer each of tortillas, beef and sauce. Then top with tortillas and sauce.

Cover both baking dishes with aluminum foil and bake in the preheated oven for 20 minutes. At the 10-minute mark, rotate each baking dish and swap which racks they are on to ensure even cooking.

Step 4:

HEARTY MINESTRONE WITH GNOCCHI

¼ cup (60 ml) olive oil

1 large yellow onion, chopped

2 ribs celery, chopped

2 carrots, chopped

While the enchilada bakes are baking, in a large Dutch oven or soup pot, heat the olive oil over medium heat. Add the chopped onion, celery and carrots and sauté until the vegetables are tender, 5 to 7 minutes.

Step 5:

HARISSA CHICKEN WITH CHARRED LEMONS AND CRISPY POTATOES

½ cup (120 ml) olive oil

4 tbsp (25 g) harissa seasoning

4 cloves garlic, minced

Zest from 1 lemon

¼ cup (60 ml) lemon juice

1 tsp salt

¼ tsp black pepper

2 lbs (907 g) bone-in, skin-on chicken thighs (about 8 thighs)

While the minestrone vegetables are cooking, make the harissa marinade. In a small bowl, combine the olive oil, harissa seasoning, minced garlic, lemon zest and juice, salt and pepper. Whisk to combine.

In a large bowl, pour the marinade over the chicken thighs and stir to coat. Divide the chicken and marinade into two portions, then place each portion into a resealable bag and press out the air. Place one portion in the refrigerator for cook night (Note: If it will be more than 2 days before you cook the chicken, place in the freezer). Place the other portion in the freezer for reheat night.

Step 6:

HEARTY MINESTRONE WITH GNOCCHI

4 cloves garlic, minced

1 tsp dried oregano

1 tsp dried thyme

1 tsp dried basil

2 russet potatoes, peeled and diced into ½-inch (1.3-cm) cubes

1 small squash, cut into ¼-inch (6-mm) rounds, then fourths (about 1 cup [113 g])

1 small zucchini, cut into ¼-inch (6-mm) rounds, then fourths (about 1 cup [113 g])

1 (14.5-oz [411-g]) can green beans, drained (or 3 cups [375 g] fresh)

1 (28-oz [794-g]) can fire-roasted diced tomatoes

6 cups (1.4 L) vegetable broth

After you have made the harissa marinade, return to the minestrone vegetables. Once the vegetables are tender, add the garlic, oregano, thyme and basil and sauté until fragrant, about 1 more minute. Add the potatoes, squash, zucchini, green beans, diced tomatoes and vegetable broth and bring to a boil. Reduce to a simmer, cover and let cook for 25 to 30 minutes, until the potatoes are tender.

SAUCY SCALLION MEATBALLS WITH ASIAN GREEN BEANS

2 lbs (907 g) ground beef

1 bunch scallions (white and green parts), thinly sliced

1 bunch cilantro, leaves finely chopped

2 eggs, gently whisked

¼ cup (60 ml) toasted sesame oil

¼ cup (60 ml) coconut aminos

⅓ cup (18 g) Paleo-friendly panko bread crumbs

While the minestrone is simmering, make the scallion meatballs by combining all the ingredients in a large bowl and mixing until well combined. Line a sheet pan with parchment paper and, using a small cookie scoop or a large spoon, scoop out the meat and roll it into golf ball–sized balls—you should make approximately 24 meatballs. Line the meatballs along the sheet tray.

Step 8:

MAKE-AHEAD ENCHILADA BAKE

Next, after the enchiladas have cooked for 20 minutes, remove the foil and bake for an additional 10 minutes.

Step 9:

HEARTY MINESTRONE WITH GNOCCHI

While the enchilada bakes are still cooking, return to the minestrone. Once the potatoes are tender, remove the soup from the heat and allow it to cool completely. Divide the soup into two equal portions, then pour each portion into an airtight container. Place one container in the refrigerator for cook night and the other in the freezer for reheat night.

Step 10:

MAKE-AHEAD ENCHILADA BAKE

After storing the minestrone, remove both enchilada bakes from the oven and let cool.

Cover both baking dishes with airtight lids or a layer of plastic wrap covered with a layer of aluminum foil and store one in the refrigerator for cook night and the other one in the freezer for reheat night.

Step 11:

SAUCY SCALLION MEATBALLS WITH ASIAN GREEN BEANS

After storing your enchilada bakes, increase the oven temperature to 400°F (204°C). Bake the meatballs for 15 to 20 minutes, until browned and cooked through (you can check using an instant-read thermometer—the internal temperature should read 160°F [71°C]). Let the meatballs cool completely, then divide them into two equal portions. Add each portion to an airtight container. Store one in the refrigerator for cook night and the other in the freezer for reheat night.

JAMAICAN JERK CHICKEN BOWLS

Serves 4 on cook night and 4 on reheat night with the additional fresh ingredients found in the reheat grocery list on page 189

I could put jerk seasoning on just about anything. Using chicken thighs for these bowls allows the meat to stay incredibly juicy. While the jerk chicken packs a serious punch, the mango-pineapple salsa does just the trick to balance out the flavors. This Caribbean cauliflower rice keeps things sweet and spicy with ginger and coconut sugar. It's a great way to add variety to traditional cauliflower rice.

½ recipe jamaican jerk chicken from the weekly prep (page 174)

1 (16-oz [454-g]) container mango-pineapple salsa

CARIBBEAN CAULIFLOWER RICE

1 tbsp (15 g) ghee

1 tsp fresh ginger, minced

1 clove garlic, minced

6 cups (680 g) frozen cauli-flower rice

1½ cups (360 ml) coconut milk

1 tbsp (15 g) coconut sugar

1 tsp salt, or to taste

PREP DAY:

See page 174 for the prep ingredients and instructions.

COOK NIGHT:

Remove the chicken from the refrigerator.

To make the cauliflower rice, in a large pot, heat the ghee over medium heat. Add the ginger and garlic and sauté for 1 minute. Add the frozen cauliflower rice, coconut milk and coconut sugar and cook for 20 minutes, until the cauliflower rice is soft and the coconut milk has thickened. Add the salt.

Preheat a grill or a grill pan on the stovetop to medium-high heat. Add the chicken thighs and cook for 5 to 7 minutes per side or until the chicken reaches 165°F (74°C). Set it aside and let it rest for a few minutes.

Slice the chicken on the diagonal and serve with salsa and cauliflower rice.

REHEAT NIGHT:

To thaw the chicken thighs in marinade overnight, move them from the freezer to the refrigerator the night before reheat night. To thaw day of, move the container from the freezer to your countertop and allow the chicken in marinade to completely thaw at room temperature. For a quick thaw, submerge the container in room temperature water until completely thawed. Once thawed, follow all of the cook and serving instructions above.

NOTE: If you'd prefer to make the jerk seasoning and salsa from scratch, see page 237 for the Jerk Seasoning recipe and page 237 for the Mango-Pineapple Salsa recipe.

SAUCY SCALLION MEATBALLS WITH ASIAN GREEN BEANS

Serves 4 on cook night and 4 on reheat night with the additional fresh ingredients found in the reheat grocery list on page 189

These scallion meatballs are bursting with flavor. I love them so much that I made them like little appetizers and kept them in a crock pot while hosting a football game. The homemade teriyaki sauce is a game changer, so be sure to check out the recipe on page 226. I love it on these meatballs and just about any other protein! Bonus: It freezes really well, so it's easy to make in bulk to have on hand for a fast meal.

½ recipe meatballs from the weekly prep (page 177)

1 (8.5-oz [241-g]) jar Paleo-friendly teriyaki sauce

GREEN BEANS

3 tbsp (45 ml) coconut aminos

2 tbsp (30 ml) toasted sesame oil

Pinch of red pepper flakes

1 lb (454 g) green beans, ends trimmed

2 cloves garlic, minced

PREP DAY:

See page 177 for the prep ingredients and instructions.

COOK NIGHT:

Preheat the oven to 350°F (177°C) and remove the meatballs from the refrigerator. Line a sheet pan with parchment paper and spread the meatballs out on it. Once the oven is hot, reheat the meatballs until warmed through, 5 to 7 minutes.

Meanwhile, in a small saucepan, heat 1 cup (240 ml) of teriyaki sauce over medium heat until warm.

To make the green beans, in a small bowl, mix together the coconut aminos, sesame oil and red pepper flakes. Preheat a skillet on the stovetop over medium-high heat. Add the green beans and then pour the sauce over them. (Be careful not to splatter, since the pan will be hot.) Stir to coat and sauté for 5 minutes. Add the minced garlic and sauté for 1 more minute.

Remove the meatballs from the oven and toss with the teriyaki sauce. Serve with the green beans.

REHEAT NIGHT:

To thaw the meatballs overnight, move them from the freezer to the refrigerator the night before reheat night. To thaw day of, move the container from the freezer to your countertop and allow the meatballs to completely thaw at room temperature. For a quick thaw, submerge the container in room temperature water until completely thawed. Once thawed, follow all of the cook and serving instructions above.

NOTE: If you'd prefer to make the sauce from scratch, see page 226 for the Teriyaki Sauce recipe.

HEARTY MINESTRONE WITH GNOCCHI

Serves 4 on cook night and 4 on reheat night with the additional fresh ingredients found in the reheat grocery list on page 189

One of my favorite experiences of my entire life was living in the Tuscan hilltop town of Cortona, Italy, in the summer of 2010. I studied abroad and got to take photography and painting lessons in Italy—it truly was the dream! I was actually a vegetarian at the time, which is where my love for minestrone originates. Even since transitioning to a Paleo diet (and feeling much better!), I still enjoy keeping my favorite meat-free meals in my rotation. This soup is full of veggies, and you will *love* the gnocchi. I hope this transports you to the hilltops of Italy as it does for me.

½ recipe minestrone from the weekly prep (page 175)

Salt and pepper, to taste

1 (12-oz [340-g]) box Paleo-friendly gnocchi

PREP DAY:

See page 175 for the prep ingredients and instructions.

COOK NIGHT:

Remove the soup from the refrigerator and pour it into a Dutch oven or soup pot on the stovetop. Reheat it over medium heat. Once the soup reaches a simmer, season with salt and pepper to taste, add the gnocchi and simmer, uncovered, for an additional 5 minutes until the gnocchi is warm and tender. Serve immediately.

REHEAT NIGHT:

To thaw the minestrone overnight, move it from the freezer to the refrigerator the night before reheat night. To thaw day of, move the container from the freezer to your countertop and allow the minestrone to completely thaw at room temperature. For a quick thaw, submerge the container in room temperature water until completely thawed. Once thawed, follow all of the cook and serving instructions above.

HARISSA CHICKEN WITH CHARRED LEMONS AND CRISPY POTATOES

Serves 4 on cook night and 4 on reheat night with the additional fresh ingredients found in the reheat grocery list on page 189

Harissa is a North African chile paste or seasoning blend with boatloads of flavor. Most harissa pastes contain questionable ingredients, so this recipe calls for a harissa seasoning instead. But trust me, you'll still get the full effect! The charred lemons brighten up this dish, and you can double this harissa marinade to make a delicious sauce for your crispy potatoes.

½ recipe harissa chicken from the weekly prep (page 175)

2 lbs (907 g) baby red or yellow potatoes

2 lemons, sliced into ¼-inch (6-mm) circles

¼ cup (60 ml) olive oil, plus more for greasing

2 cloves garlic, minced

1 tbsp (2 g) fresh rosemary, finely chopped

Salt and pepper, to taste

PREP DAY:

See page 175 for the prep ingredients and instructions.

COOK NIGHT:

If your marinated chicken is frozen, be sure to thaw it at room temperature completely beforehand. To thaw even more quickly, you can place the chicken in a sealed bag in warm water.

Preheat the oven to 425°F (218°C).

Put the potatoes in a large pot and cover them with water. Bring the water to a rolling boil on the stovetop and cook the potatoes until tender, 15 to 20 minutes.

While the potatoes are cooking, spread out the chicken thighs and lemon slices in a shallow baking dish and place in the oven to cook for 15 minutes.

Meanwhile, prepare a sheet pan for the potatoes by lightly coating it with olive oil or avocado oil cooking spray. Drain the potatoes and transfer them to the sheet tray. Using a fork or a potato masher, mash each potato until flattened.

In a small bowl, whisk together the olive oil, garlic, rosemary and salt and pepper to taste. Drizzle the liquid over the smashed potatoes.

When the chicken has cooked for 20 minutes, add the potatoes to the oven as well and cook both the potatoes and chicken for an additional 20 minutes, until the chicken has cooked through and the potatoes are crispy.

Serve the chicken thighs with the charred lemons and crispy potatoes.

REHEAT NIGHT:

Remove the chicken in the marinade from the freezer and thaw completely at room temperature.

Follow the instructions for cook night.

MAKE-AHEAD ENCHILADA BAKE

Serves 4 on cook night and 4 on reheat night with the additional fresh ingredients found in the reheat grocery list on page 189

I will make this enchilada bake over and over again for the rest of my life, and with pleasure. You know Mexican food is my absolute favorite, and I especially adore this enchilada bake because you make both dishes on prep day, so all you have to do is pull it out of the freezer, cook it and eat it! The homemade version of this enchilada sauce on page 237 is worth making when you have the time. I literally make a quadruple batch and freeze the extra to have on hand. For serving, go crazy on the toppings with this one—I essentially turn it into a salad.

½ recipe enchilada bake from the weekly prep (page 174)

TOPPINGS

1 head iceberg lettuce, thinly sliced

2 avocados, sliced

2 Roma tomatoes, diced

½ red onion, chopped

PREP DAY:

See page 174 for the prep ingredients and instructions.

COOK NIGHT:

Remove the enchilada bake from the refrigerator and let it stand at room temperature for 30 minutes while preheating the oven to 350°F (177°C). Remove the lid or plastic and aluminum foil and re-cover with just the aluminum foil. Heat it in the oven until warmed through, about 20 minutes.

Remove it from the oven, cut the enchilada bake into fourths and plate it with the desired toppings.

REHEAT NIGHT:

To thaw the enchilada bake, move it from the freezer to the refrigerator the night before reheat night, giving it adequate time to completely thaw. Once thawed, follow the instructions from cook night.

NOTE: If you'd prefer to make the sauce from scratch, see page 237 for the Enchilada Sauce recipe.

WEEK 10 GROCERY LIST

PROTEIN

- [ ] 2 lbs (907 g) boneless, skinless chicken thighs •
- [ ] 2 lbs (907 g) bone-in, skin-on chicken thighs •
- [ ] 4 lbs (1.8 kg) ground beef • •
- [ ] 2 eggs •

PRODUCE

- [ ] Lime juice •
- [ ] ¼ cup (60 ml) lemon juice •
- [ ] 1 Scotch bonnet pepper (or jalapeño) •
- [ ] 1 bunch cilantro •
- [ ] Fresh ginger •
- [ ] 2 heads garlic • • • • •
- [ ] 1 bunch scallions •
- [ ] 1 lb (454 g) green beans •
- [ ] 2 yellow onions • •
- [ ] 2 ribs celery •
- [ ] 2 carrots •
- [ ] 2 russet potatoes •
- [ ] 1 yellow squash •
- [ ] 1 zucchini •
- [ ] 3 lemons •
- [ ] 2 lbs (907 g) baby red or yellow potatoes •
- [ ] 1 bunch rosemary •
- [ ] 2 sweet potatoes •
- [ ] 1 red bell pepper •
- [ ] 1 yellow bell pepper •
- [ ] 1 orange bell pepper •
- [ ] 1 head iceberg lettuce •
- [ ] 2 avocados •
- [ ] 2 Roma tomatoes •
- [ ] 1 red onion •

SPICES

- [ ] Dried thyme •
- [ ] Red pepper flakes •
- [ ] Dried oregano •
- [ ] Dried basil •
- [ ] Harissa seasoning •

- [ ] Jerk seasoning mix (I like Primal Palate Jerk Seasoning) •

PANTRY

- [ ] Coconut sugar •
- [ ] 1 (13.5-oz [398-ml]) can coconut milk •
- [ ] ½ cup (120 ml) toasted sesame oil •
- [ ] ½ cup (120 ml) coconut aminos •
- [ ] ⅓ cup (18 g) Paleo-friendly panko bread crumbs (I like Jeff Nathan Creations Chef Gourmet Panko Plain Gluten Free) •
- [ ] 1 (14.5-oz [411-g]) can green beans •
- [ ] 1 (28-oz [794-g]) can fire-roasted diced tomatoes •
- [ ] 2 (32-oz [960-ml]) boxes vegetable broth •
- [ ] 1 (8.5-oz [241-g]) jar Paleo-friendly teriyaki sauce (I like Primal Kitchen No-Soy Teriyaki Sauce & Marinade) •
- [ ] 4½ cups (1.1 L) Paleo-friendly enchilada sauce (I like Siete Red Enchilada Sauce) •
- [ ] 1 (16-oz [454-g]) container mango-pineapple salsa (I like Stonewall Kitchen Mango Lime Salsa, or get a container of fresh-made salsa from the grocery store) •

FREEZER

- [ ] 6 cups (680 g) frozen cauliflower rice •
- [ ] 1 (12-oz [340-g]) box frozen Paleo-friendly gnocchi (I like Cappello's, found in the freezer section) •
- [ ] 3 (8-piece) frozen packages taco-sized grain-free tortillas (I like Siete Cassava Tortillas) •

DAIRY ALTERNATIVES

- [ ] Unsalted ghee (I like Fourth & Heart) •

RECIPES KEY: • • • • •

Jamaican Jerk Chicken Bowls (page 178)
Saucy Scallion Meatballs with Asian Green Beans (page 181)
Harissa Chicken with Charred Lemons and Crispy Potatoes (page 185)
Hearty Minestrone with Gnocchi (page 182)
Make-Ahead Enchilada Bake (page 186)

WEEK 10 REHEAT GROCERY LIST

JAMAICAN JERK CHICKEN BOWLS

- ☐ 1 (16-oz [454-g]) container mango-pineapple salsa (I like Stonewall Kitchen Mango Lime Salsa, or get a container of fresh-made salsa from the grocery)
- ☐ Fresh ginger
- ☐ 1 clove garlic
- ☐ 6 cups (680 g) frozen cauliflower rice
- ☐ 1 (13.5-oz [398-ml]) can coconut milk
- ☐ Coconut sugar
- ☐ Unsalted ghee (I like Fourth & Heart)

SAUCY SCALLION MEATBALLS WITH ASIAN GREEN BEANS

- ☐ 1 lb (454 g) green beans
- ☐ Coconut aminos
- ☐ Toasted sesame oil
- ☐ 2 cloves garlic
- ☐ Red pepper flakes
- ☐ 1 (8.5-oz [241-g]) jar Paleo-friendly teriyaki sauce (I like Primal Kitchen No-Soy Teriyaki Sauce & Marinade)

HEARTY MINESTRONE WITH GNOCCHI

- ☐ 1 (12-oz [340-g]) box Paleo-friendly gnocchi (I like Cappello's Gnocchi)

HARISSA CHICKEN WITH CHARRED LEMONS AND CRISPY POTATOES

- ☐ 2 lemons
- ☐ 2 lbs (907 g) baby red or yellow potatoes
- ☐ 1 bunch rosemary
- ☐ 2 cloves garlic

MAKE-AHEAD ENCHILADA BAKE

- ☐ 1 head iceberg lettuce
- ☐ 2 avocados
- ☐ 2 Roma tomatoes
- ☐ 1 red onion

WEEK 11

I'm a huge fan of lamb and think we should incorporate it into our diets more often! Just like beef stew meat, lamb stew meat is the perfect introduction to cooking lamb because it's already cut when you buy it and it's easy to toss into recipes. If you can't easily find lamb, you can replace it with beef stew meat in both recipes. The Paleo hummus is delicious with the lamb ragù and pine nut tabbouleh. Be sure to make my cauliflower hummus recipe on page 238—it makes for a great afternoon snack with veggies. The mustard pork tenderloin is fast and easy but tastes incredibly gourmet. It's the perfect combination for hosting a dinner party. The "cheddar" we use in the broccoli "cheddar" soup and the loaded mashed potatoes is next-level good!

WEEK 11 PREP-DAY INSTRUCTIONS

If you've never attempted to cook pork tenderloins, these two recipes are a great start. The meat stays perfectly moist by cooking the mustard pork tenderloins in a Dutch oven and wrapping the other pork tenderloins in bacon. I'm also excited for you to cook lamb this week! Cooking lamb stew meat couldn't be simpler. The pomegranate lamb is easy to roast low and slow in a Dutch oven. Meanwhile, the lamb ragù is equally easy to cook in the Instant Pot or on the stovetop. You'll love making the "cheddar" for both the soup and the loaded mashed potatoes. It's such a tasty, dairy-free rendition of the classic.

Step 1:

MUSTARD PORK TENDERLOIN WITH SWEET POTATO LATKES

2 (1-lb [454-g]) pork tenderloins

6 cloves garlic

2 tbsp (30 ml) Dijon mustard

2 tbsp (3 g) fresh rosemary, chopped (or 1½ tsp [2 g] dried)

1 tsp lemon zest

1 tbsp (18 g) kosher salt

1 tsp black pepper

2 tbsp (30 ml) olive oil, divided

To make the mustard pork tenderloin, first preheat the oven to 300°F (149°C).

Trim any excess fat and silver skin from each tenderloin.

In a large bowl, combine the garlic, mustard, rosemary, lemon zest, salt, pepper and olive oil. Add both pork tenderloins to the bowl or a large resealable bag and coat well with the marinade. Cover the bowl (or seal the bag) and let the pork sit in the marinade in the refrigerator.

Step 2:

POMEGRANATE LAMB OVER MASHED BUTTERNUT SQUASH

2 tbsp (30 ml) olive oil

2 lbs (907 g) lamb stew meat

2 tsp (12 g) salt

1 tsp black pepper

1 (12-oz [340-g]) jar Paleo-friendly muhammara simmer sauce

1 tbsp (6 g) fresh mint leaves, chopped

While the mustard pork tenderloin is marinating, adjust your oven racks to accommodate the Dutch oven for the lamb.

In a large Dutch oven, heat the olive oil. Season the lamb with the salt and pepper, and then add the lamb (in batches if necessary so as not to crowd the pan) and brown the meat on all sides, 5 to 7 minutes. Add the simmer sauce and chopped mint and stir to combine.

Cover with the lid, place in the preheated oven and cook for 2 hours, or until the lamb is fork-tender.

Step 3:

LAMB RAGÙ WITH CAULIFLOWER HUMMUS AND PINE NUT TABBOULEH

2 lbs (907 g) lamb stew meat

1 tsp salt, plus more for seasoning

½ tsp black pepper, plus more for seasoning

2 tbsp (30 ml) olive oil

4 shallots, sliced into ¼-inch (6-mm) circles

2 cloves garlic, minced

2 cups (480 ml) beef bone broth, divided

1 (15-oz [425-g]) can tomato sauce

1 tbsp (6 g) cumin

While the pomegranate lamb is cooking, season the lamb for the ragù with salt and pepper. Set an Instant Pot to the sauté setting and, when hot, add the olive oil (or skip ahead for stovetop instructions). Add the lamb (working in batches if needed) and sear the meat. Remove it from the pot and set it aside. Add the shallots to the Instant Pot and sauté until tender, about 2 minutes. Add the garlic and sauté until fragrant, about 1 more minute. Pour ½ cup (120 ml) of the beef bone broth to deglaze the pot and loosen up any browned bits with a spatula. Turn the Instant Pot off and add the lamb back to the pot. Add the tomato sauce, cumin, additional salt to taste and the remaining broth.

Seal the pot and set to the Meat/Stew setting for 45 minutes. When the timer goes off, allow the vent to naturally release for at least 10 minutes.

If you do not have an Instant Pot, heat the olive oil in a large Dutch oven or stew pot over medium heat. Season the lamb with salt and pepper and add it to the pot. Sear the meat until it is browned on all sides, 5 to 7 minutes. Remove the meat from the pot and set it aside. Add the shallots and garlic and sauté until tender and fragrant, about 3 minutes. Add ½ cup (120 ml) of the bone broth and scrape the browned bits from the bottom of the pot. Return the lamb to the pot and add the remaining bone broth, tomato sauce, and cumin, as well as additional salt and pepper to taste. Bring to a boil, then reduce the heat to a simmer, cover and cook for 1½ to 2 hours, until the lamb is very tender.

Step 4:

CREAMY BROCCOLI "CHEDDAR" SOUP

1½ cups (341 g) unsalted ghee

3 large onions, chopped

4 cloves garlic, minced

3 cups (438 g) raw cashews

3 cups (405 g) pine nuts

3 tbsp (21 g) paprika

¼ cup (20 g) nutritional yeast

1½ tbsp (27 g) salt

2 tsp (4 g) black pepper

1½ tsp (9 g) turmeric

3 (13.5-oz [398-ml]) cans coconut milk, divided

1½ tbsp (22 ml) lemon juice

1 cup (240 ml) vegetable broth

8 cups (568 g) broccoli, chopped (approximately 2 large heads)

Note that you are making double the "cheddar" part for the loaded mashed potatoes (page 204), so if you are just making this recipe and not the whole week, halve the cheddar ingredients.

While the lamb for the lamb ragù is cooking, start working on the soup. In a large pot or Dutch oven over medium-high heat, melt the ghee. Add the onions and sauté until translucent, about 5 minutes. Add the garlic and sauté until fragrant, about 1 minute more.

Add the cashews and pine nuts and sauté for 5 minutes. Add the paprika, nutritional yeast, salt, pepper and turmeric. Stir thoroughly to coat the cashews and pine nuts and sauté for an additional 2 minutes.

Pour all of the contents of the pot into a blender and add 1 can of coconut milk and the lemon juice. (If your blender is not big enough, you can do this step in batches. Feel free to add as much of the other 2 cans of coconut milk here as is necessary to blend.) Blend until smooth.

Return the blender contents to the pot on the stovetop. Add the remaining cans of coconut milk and the vegetable broth and stir to combine.

Reserve 2 cups (480 ml) of this "cheddar" mixture for your loaded mashed potatoes in a small mixing bowl or storage container.

Add the chopped broccoli to the pot with the "cheddar" mixture, cover and simmer until the broccoli is tender, 15 to 20 minutes. Add more vegetable broth if needed to thin out the soup and let simmer.

Step 5:

POMEGRANATE LAMB OVER MASHED BUTTERNUT SQUASH

2 tbsp (30 ml) olive oil

2 (10-oz [283-g]) bags frozen butternut squash

2 cloves garlic, minced

1 (13.5-oz [398-ml]) can coconut milk

Salt and pepper, to taste

While the soup cooks, heat the olive oil in a large skillet over medium heat. Add the butternut squash and sauté until the squash is tender and beginning to caramelize, about 10 minutes. Add the minced garlic and sauté until fragrant, about 1 minute more. Remove the pot from the heat and, in a large mixing bowl, combine the squash and coconut milk. Using an electric mixer or potato masher, blend the ingredients until smooth. Season to taste with salt and pepper. Allow the mash to cool completely and divide it into two equal portions. Place both portions into airtight containers. Put one portion in the refrigerator for cook night and the other portion in the freezer for reheat night.

Step 6:

CREAMY BROCCOLI "CHEDDAR" SOUP

After storing the butternut squash, the soup should be finished cooking. Allow the soup to cool completely. Divide it into two equal portions in airtight containers. Store one portion in the refrigerator for cook night and the other portion in the freezer for reheat night.

Step 7:

MUSTARD PORK TENDERLOIN WITH SWEET POTATO LATKES

½ cup (120 g) fresh horseradish, grated

½ cup (120 ml) Paleo-friendly mayonnaise

While the Instant Pot is naturally releasing for the lamb ragù, make the horseradish sauce by combining the grated horseradish and mayonnaise in a blender or food processor and blend until smooth. Store in an airtight container in the refrigerator.

Step 8:

BACON-WRAPPED PORK TENDERLOIN WITH LOADED MASHED POTATOES

2 (1-lb [454-g]) pork tenderloins

1 tsp salt

1 tsp black pepper

2 (8-oz [226-g]) packages Paleo-friendly bacon

After making and storing the horseradish sauce, begin working on the bacon-wrapped pork tenderloin. Season both tenderloins with salt and pepper. Wrap each pork tenderloin in bacon, one piece at a time. Be sure to overlap each piece of bacon so that it stays together. Place both wrapped pork tenderloins in an oven-safe baking dish and set aside.

Step 9:

POMEGRANATE LAMB OVER MASHED BUTTERNUT SQUASH

Once the lamb has cooked, remove it from the oven and allow it to cool completely. Increase your oven temperature to 400°F (204°C). Divide the cooled pomegranate lamb into two equal portions. Place both portions into airtight containers. Put one portion in the refrigerator for cook night and the other portion in the freezer for reheat night.

Step 10:

BACON-WRAPPED PORK TENDERLOIN WITH LOADED MASHED POTATOES

1 (8-oz [226-g]) package Paleo-friendly bacon

After storing the pomegranate lamb, cook the bacon for the loaded mashed potatoes. Place the bacon slices on a parchment paper–lined sheet pan. Put the bacon in the 400°F (204°C) heated oven and cook for 10 to 12 minutes, until it's crispy. Set it aside to cool.

Place the tray of bacon-wrapped pork tenderloins into the 400°F (204°C) oven for 30 minutes, or until the bacon is crispy and an instant-read thermometer inserted into the center of the pork tenderloin reads at least 145°F (63°C). Transfer the pork to a cutting board and let it rest.

Step 11:

MUSTARD PORK TENDERLOIN WITH SWEET POTATO LATKES

2 tbsp (30 ml) olive oil

While the bacon-wrapped pork tenderloin is cooking, remove the marinating tenderloins from the refrigerator. Heat the olive oil in a large ovenproof skillet over medium-high heat. Sear both tenderloins on both sides, about 4 minutes each side.

Transfer the pork in the skillet to the oven alongside the bacon-wrapped pork tenderloins and roast until an instant-read thermometer inserted into the thickest part of the pork registers 145°F (63°C), 15 to 20 minutes. Transfer the pork to a cutting board and let rest.

Step 12:

BACON-WRAPPED PORK TENDERLOIN WITH LOADED MASHED POTATOES

6 russet potatoes

1 tbsp (18 g) kosher salt, plus more to taste

¼ cup (57 g) unsalted ghee

½ cup (120 ml) unsweetened plain Paleo-friendly yogurt

1 tsp black pepper

2 cups (480 ml) remaining "cheddar" mixture from the Creamy Broccoli "Cheddar" Soup

Wash and chop the potatoes into large chunks. I prefer to leave the skins on, but you can peel them before chopping. Fill a large pot with water on the stovetop and add the potatoes and the salt. Bring the water with the potatoes to a gentle boil and cook uncovered until the potatoes are fork-tender, 15 to 20 minutes.

While the potatoes are boiling, chop the crispy bacon from step 10 into small pieces. Drain the potatoes and transfer them to a large stand mixer fitted with the paddle attachment. Add the ghee, yogurt, additional salt to taste and pepper and mix on low speed until well combined. Add the "cheddar" mixture ½ cup (120 ml) at a time until the full amount is added. Add the chopped bacon and adjust the seasonings (if needed). Divide the loaded potatoes into two equal portions. Store one portion in an airtight container in the refrigerator for cook night and the other portion in an airtight container in the freezer for reheat night.

Step 13:

MUSTARD PORK TENDERLOIN WITH SWEET POTATO LATKES

After storing the loaded mashed potatoes, return to the mustard pork tenderloin. Once all of the tenderloins have cooled, wrap one mustard tenderloin and one bacon-wrapped tenderloin in plastic wrap or put into an airtight container and freeze for reheat week. Wrap the other mustard tenderloin and bacon-wrapped tenderloin in airtight containers and store them both in the refrigerator.

LAMB RAGÙ WITH CAULIFLOWER HUMMUS AND PINE NUT TABBOULEH

Serves 4 on cook night and 4 on reheat night with the additional fresh ingredients found in the reheat grocery list on page 207

This meal is inspired by a local Denver restaurant that serves modern Israeli cuisine. My favorite dish there is their hummus with short rib on top. The combination of Instant Pot ragù and store-bought Paleo hummus makes this a super quick but impressively gourmet recipe. The homemade cauliflower hummus on page 238 is divine, and whichever hummus you choose, the lamb ragù is absolutely phenomenal. Replacing the bulgur in traditional tabbouleh with pine nuts makes it grain free and Paleo friendly. You can replace the lamb stew meat with beef stew meat, if you prefer.

½ recipe lamb ragù from the weekly prep (page 192)

2 (8-oz [226-g]) containers Paleo-friendly cauliflower hummus

2 tbsp (8 g) parsley, chopped, for garnish (optional)

TABBOULEH

⅓ cup (45 g) pine nuts

3 cups (108 g) fresh flat-leaf parsley, chopped

¼ cup (23 g) fresh mint, chopped

1 pint (510 g) cherry tomatoes, quartered

1 bunch scallions, finely chopped

¼ cup (60 ml) olive oil

1 clove garlic, minced

3 tbsp (44 ml) lemon juice

Salt and pepper, to taste

PREP DAY:

See page 192 for the prep ingredients and instructions.

COOK NIGHT:

Reheat the lamb ragù in a pot on the stovetop over medium heat, about 10 minutes.

Meanwhile, make the tabbouleh. In a medium bowl, combine the pine nuts, parsley, mint, tomatoes and scallions.

In a small bowl, whisk together the olive oil, minced garlic, lemon juice and salt and pepper to taste.

Pour the dressing over the tabbouleh and stir to combine.

Serve the lamb ragù over a large dollop of the cauliflower hummus and with a side of tabbouleh. Garnish with the parsley, if desired.

REHEAT NIGHT:

To thaw the lamb ragù overnight, move it from the freezer to the refrigerator the night before reheat night. To thaw day of, move the container from the freezer to your countertop and allow the ragù to completely thaw at room temperature. For a quick thaw, submerge the container in room temperature water until completely thawed. Once thawed, follow the cook night instructions.

NOTE: If you'd prefer to make the hummus from scratch, see page 238 for the Cauliflower Hummus recipe.

CREAMY BROCCOLI "CHEDDAR" SOUP

Serves 4 on cook night and 4 on reheat night

How on earth can cheddar soup be made dairy-free? Well, my friends, just try this recipe. I love the "cheese" so much that I use it in all sorts of different recipes. You'll notice it's even used for the loaded mashed potatoes (page 204) you'll be having later this week.

½ recipe broccoli "cheddar" soup from the weekly prep (page 193)

1 cup (240 ml) vegetable broth, if needed

Salt and pepper, to taste

PREP DAY:

See page 193 for the prep ingredients and instructions.

COOK NIGHT:

Remove the soup from the refrigerator and pour it into a soup pot on the stovetop. Reheat the soup over medium heat until warmed through, 8 to 10 minutes. Add more vegetable broth if necessary to thin out the soup. Season to taste with salt and pepper and serve hot.

REHEAT NIGHT:

To thaw the soup overnight, move it from the freezer to the refrigerator the night before reheat night. To thaw day of, move the container from the freezer to your countertop and allow the soup to completely thaw at room temperature. For a quick thaw, submerge the container in room temperature water until completely thawed. Once thawed, follow the cook night instructions.

MUSTARD PORK TENDERLOIN WITH SWEET POTATO LATKES

Serves 4 on cook night and 4 on reheat night with the additional fresh ingredients found in the reheat grocery list on page 207

When I first made this, Chaz said it was the best recipe I've made for him *ever*. The garlic cloves caramelize while the pork tenderloin is roasting, and we fight over who gets to eat them! This horseradish sauce is the easiest sauce you will ever make, and it goes great with both the pork tenderloin and sweet potato latkes.

1 mustard pork tenderloin from the weekly prep (page 192)

1 tbsp (15 ml) olive oil

Horseradish sauce from the weekly prep (page 194)

SWEET POTATO LATKES

1 lb (454 g) sweet potatoes, peeled and coarsely grated

2 scallions, finely chopped

⅓ cup (41 g) cassava flour

2 large eggs, lightly beaten

1 tsp salt

½ tsp black pepper

¾ cup (180 ml) light olive oil or avocado oil, plus more to coat the pan

HORSERADISH SAUCE (FOR REHEAT NIGHT)

½ cup (120 g) fresh horseradish, grated

½ cup (120 ml) Paleo-friendly mayonnaise

PREP DAY:

See page 192 for the prep ingredients and instructions.

COOK NIGHT:

Remove the pork tenderloin from the refrigerator.

Find a pan with a lid that will hold the whole pork tenderloin. Coat the bottom of the pan with olive oil, and heat over medium heat until the oil is shimmering. Add the pork tenderloin and cover immediately with the lid. Cook on medium-low heat for 10 to 12 minutes, flipping every few minutes, until warmed through.

While the pork tenderloin is reheating, make the latkes. Stir together the sweet potatoes, scallions, cassava flour, eggs, salt and pepper.

Heat the ¾ cup (180 ml) of oil in a deep 12-inch (30-cm) nonstick skillet or Dutch oven over medium-high heat until hot. Working in batches of four, spoon ¼ cup (60 ml) of the potato mixture per latke into the oil and flatten it to 3-inch (7.5-cm) diameter with a slotted spatula. Reduce the heat to medium and cook until golden, about 1½ minutes on each side. Transfer the latkes with a spatula to paper towels to drain.

Slice the pork and serve with the latkes and horseradish sauce.

REHEAT NIGHT:

To thaw the pork tenderloin overnight, move it from the freezer to the refrigerator the night before reheat night. To thaw day of, move the container from the freezer to your countertop and allow the pork to completely thaw at room temperature. For a quick thaw, submerge the container in room temperature water until completely thawed.

Make a fresh batch of the horseradish sauce by combining the grated horseradish and mayonnaise in a blender or food processor and blend until smooth. Once your pork tenderloin is thawed, follow the cook night instructions.

POMEGRANATE LAMB OVER MASHED BUTTERNUT SQUASH

Serves 4 on cook night and 4 on reheat night with the additional fresh ingredients found in the reheat grocery list on page 207

This recipe makes me wonder why I didn't cook with pomegranate more often before now! The combination of pomegranate and mint provides such a unique flavor for this lamb dish. The mashed butternut squash is such a lovely, rich side dish that I make frequently. If you have the time, it's worth getting a fresh butternut squash to roast for depth of flavor. You can replace the lamb stew meat with beef stew meat, if you prefer.

½ recipe pomegranate lamb from the weekly prep (page 192)

½ recipe mashed butternut squash from the weekly prep (page 194)

2 tbsp (30 ml) coconut milk, if needed

2 tbsp (12 g) fresh mint leaves, chopped, divided (half for garnish, optional)

¼ cup (35 g) pomegranate seeds, for garnish

PREP DAY:

See page 192 for the prep ingredients and instructions.

COOK NIGHT:

Remove the lamb and the mashed butternut squash from the refrigerator. Put the lamb in a large pot on the stovetop and reheat over medium heat until warmed through, 8 to 10 minutes. Put the mashed squash in a medium pot on the stovetop and reheat over medium heat until warmed through, 8 to 10 minutes (adding a few tablespoons [30 ml] of coconut milk if necessary). Once the lamb and squash are reheated, serve the lamb over a large dollop of squash and garnish with chopped mint and pomegranate seeds.

REHEAT NIGHT:

To thaw the lamb and squash overnight, move them from the freezer to the refrigerator the night before reheat night. To thaw day of, move each container from the freezer to your countertop and allow the lamb and squash to completely thaw at room temperature. For a quick thaw, submerge each container in room temperature water until completely thawed. Once thawed, follow the cook night instructions.

NOTE: If you prefer to make a homemade version of this pomegranate lamb, see page 238 for that recipe.

BACON-WRAPPED PORK TENDERLOIN WITH LOADED MASHED POTATOES

Serves 4 on cook night and 4 on reheat night with the additional fresh ingredients found in the reheat grocery list on page 207

Anytime you wrap bacon around something, you know it's going to be good. This bacon-wrapped pork tenderloin is no exception. These loaded mashed potatoes taste just like twice-baked potatoes, but in mashed potato form. If you find yourself meandering over to the refrigerator to snag a bite of these potatoes, I won't judge. I've done it, too.

1 bacon-wrapped pork tenderloin from the weekly prep (page 194)

½ recipe loaded mashed potatoes from the weekly prep (page 195)

1 tbsp (15 ml) olive oil

¼ cup (60 ml) coconut milk or vegetable broth (optional)

1 bunch scallions (green parts only), chopped, for garnish (optional)

SIMPLE ARUGULA SALAD

1 (5-oz [141-g]) package arugula

1 (5.07-oz [144-g]) bottle Paleo-friendly fig balsamic glaze

> **NOTE:** If you'd prefer to make the fig balsamic glaze from scratch, see page 239 for the recipe.

PREP DAY:

See pages 194 and 195 for the prep ingredients and instructions.

COOK NIGHT:

Remove the pork tenderloin and loaded mashed potatoes from the refrigerator.

Find a pan with a lid that will hold the whole pork tenderloin. Coat the bottom of the pan with the olive oil, and heat it over medium heat until the oil is shimmering. Add the pork tenderloin and cover immediately with the lid. Cook on medium-low heat for 10 to 12 minutes, flipping every few minutes, until warmed through.

Add the loaded mashed potatoes to a saucepan on the stovetop. Cover with a lid and reheat over low heat until warmed through, 8 to 10 minutes. Add coconut milk or broth if needed to moisten the potatoes.

Once the pork is warmed through, remove it from the pan and slice it on the diagonal. Serve the pork tenderloin with a side of loaded mashed potatoes and a handful of arugula topped with the fig balsamic glaze over it and as a dipping sauce for the pork tenderloin. Garnish with the scallions, if desired.

REHEAT NIGHT:

To thaw the pork tenderloin and mashed potatoes overnight, move them from the freezer to the refrigerator the night before reheat night. To thaw day of, move each container from the freezer to your countertop and allow the pork and potatoes to completely thaw at room temperature. For a quick thaw, submerge each container in room temperature water until completely thawed. Once thawed, follow the cook night instructions.

WEEK 11 GROCERY LIST

PROTEIN

- ☐ 4 lbs (1.8 kg) lamb stew meat ● ●
- ☐ 4 (1-lb [454-g]) pork tenderloins ● ●
- ☐ 2 eggs ●
- ☐ 3 (8-oz [226-g]) packages Paleo-friendly bacon ●

PRODUCE

- ☐ 4 shallots ●
- ☐ 1 head garlic ● ● ● ●
- ☐ 2 bunches flat-leaf parsley ●
- ☐ ¼ cup (60 ml) lemon juice ● ●
- ☐ 1 bunch mint ● ●
- ☐ 1 pint (510 g) cherry tomatoes ●
- ☐ 2 bunches scallions ● ● ● ●
- ☐ 3 yellow onions ●
- ☐ 2 heads broccoli ●
- ☐ 1 bunch rosemary ●
- ☐ 1 lemon ●
- ☐ 1 lb (454 g) sweet potatoes ●
- ☐ ¼ cup (35 g) fresh pomegranate seeds ●
- ☐ 6 russet potatoes ●
- ☐ 1 (5-oz [141-g]) package arugula ●
- ☐ ½ cup (120 g) fresh horseradish ●
- ☐ 2 (8-oz [226-g]) containers Paleo-friendly hummus (I like Naya Cauliflower Hummus) ●

SPICES

- ☐ Cumin ●
- ☐ Paprika ●
- ☐ Turmeric ●

PANTRY

- ☐ 1 (15-oz [425-g]) can tomato sauce ●
- ☐ 1 (32-oz [960-ml]) box beef bone broth ●
- ☐ 3⅓ cups (450 g) pine nuts ● ●
- ☐ 3 cups (438 g) raw cashews ●
- ☐ 4 (13.5-oz [398-ml]) cans coconut milk ● ●
- ☐ ¼ cup (20 g) nutritional yeast ●
- ☐ 1 (32-oz [960-ml]) box vegetable broth ●
- ☐ Dijon mustard ●
- ☐ ½ cup (120 ml) Paleo-friendly mayonnaise ●
- ☐ Cassava flour ●
- ☐ 1 (12-oz [340-g]) jar Paleo-friendly muhammara simmer sauce (I like Chosen Foods Muhammara Red Pepper Simmer Sauce) ●
- ☐ 1 (5.07-oz [144-g]) bottle balsamic glaze (I like Sur La Table Fig Balsamic Glaze) ●

DAIRY ALTERNATIVES

- ☐ Unsalted ghee (I like Fourth & Heart) ● ●
- ☐ 1 (5.3-oz [150-g]) container unsweetened plain Paleo-friendly yogurt (I like Forager Project Unsweetened Plain Cashewmilk Yogurt) ●

FREEZER

- ☐ 2 (10-oz [283-g]) bags frozen butternut squash ●

RECIPES KEY: ● ● ● ● ●

| Lamb Ragù with Cauliflower Hummus and Pine Nut Tabbouleh (page 196) |
| Mustard Pork Tenderloin with Sweet Potato Latkes (page 200) |
| Pomegranate Lamb over Mashed Butternut Squash (page 203) |
| Creamy Broccoli "Cheddar" Soup (page 199) |
| Bacon-Wrapped Pork Tenderloin with Loaded Mashed Potatoes (page 204) |

WEEK 11 REHEAT GROCERY LIST

LAMB RAGÙ WITH CAULIFLOWER HUMMUS AND PINE NUT TABBOULEH

- [ ] 2 (8-oz [227-g]) containers Paleo-friendly hummus (I like Naya Cauliflower Hummus)
- [ ] ⅓ cup (45 g) pine nuts
- [ ] 2 bunches flat-leaf parsley
- [ ] 1 bunch mint
- [ ] 1 pint (510 g) cherry tomatoes
- [ ] Lemon juice
- [ ] 1 clove garlic

CREAMY BROCCOLI "CHEDDAR" SOUP

- [ ] Nothing needed

MUSTARD PORK TENDERLOIN WITH SWEET POTATO LATKES

- [ ] 1 lb (454 g) sweet potatoes
- [ ] 1 bunch scallions
- [ ] Cassava flour
- [ ] 2 eggs
- [ ] ½ cup (120 g) fresh horseradish
- [ ] ½ cup (120 ml) Paleo-friendly mayonnaise

POMEGRANATE LAMB OVER MASHED BUTTERNUT SQUASH

- [ ] 1 bunch mint
- [ ] ¼ cup (35 g) pomegranate seeds

BACON-WRAPPED PORK TENDERLOIN WITH LOADED MASHED POTATOES

- [ ] 1 (5-oz [141-g]) package arugula
- [ ] 1 (5.07-oz [144-g]) jar bottle balsamic glaze (I like Sur La Table Fig Balsamic Glaze)
- [ ] 1 (13.5-oz [398-ml]) can coconut milk

WEEK 12

This week has a myriad of flavors from Hawaiian, Asian, Italian, Russian and American cuisines. This Silky Beef Stroganoff is such a luxurious dish, yet it's incredibly easy to prepare. It's great to serve at a dinner party. The homemade dairy-free pesto (page 239) is so delicious that I pour it on so many things. My favorite way to use it is over veggies for breakfast. The Fast and Fresh Poke Bowls will transport you to the shores of Hawaii—just take me with you, promise?

WEEK 12 PREP-DAY INSTRUCTIONS

This is another week that relies on the ease of beef stew meat. The sesame beef can be cooked in the Instant Pot or on the stove while the beef Stroganoff is slow-roasted in a Dutch oven. Meanwhile, the pesto veggie bowls are reminiscent of my college days, and they're the best simple sheet pan meal. The tuna burgers can be made today and frozen, making for a quick meal later. Since poke bowls don't have to be cooked, they're the fastest recipe in the entire book!

Step 1:

SESAME BEEF STIR-FRY WITH BOK CHOY

2 lbs (907 g) beef stew meat

2 tbsp (16 g) arrowroot

Salt and pepper

¼ cup (60 ml) olive oil, divided

½ cup (120 ml) beef or chicken bone broth

½ to 1 cup (120 to 240 ml) Paleo-friendly sesame-ginger sauce (depending on your cooking method)

To make the sesame beef, toss the beef with the arrowroot, salt and pepper and set it aside.

Set the Instant Pot to sauté and, working in two batches, add half of the olive oil and half of the beef and brown the beef on all sides. Remove the beef from the Instant Pot and set aside.

Deglaze the Instant Pot with the beef bone broth, then turn the Instant Pot off.

Return the beef to the Instant Pot and cover with ½ cup (120 ml) of Paleo-friendly sesame-ginger sauce. Secure the lid and set the Instant Pot to Meat/Stew for 60 minutes.

If you do not have an Instant Pot, season the beef with salt and pepper, then toss it with the arrowroot and set it aside. Heat the olive oil in a large Dutch oven or stew pot over medium heat. Add the beef and sear until the meat is browned on all sides. Deglaze the pot with the bone broth. Add 1 cup (240 ml) of the sesame-ginger sauce. Bring to a boil, then reduce the heat to a simmer, cover the pot and cook for 1½ to 2 hours until the meat is tender. Check halfway through and add more bone broth if necessary.

Step 2:

SILKY BEEF STROGANOFF

2 lbs (907 g) beef stew meat

Salt and pepper

2 tbsp (30 ml) olive oil, divided

½ cup (80 g) shallots, finely chopped

3 cloves garlic, minced

2¼ cups (532 ml) beef bone broth, divided

¼ cup (60 ml) Dijon mustard

While the sesame beef is cooking, move on to the beef Stroganoff. Season the beef with salt and pepper. Heat 1 tablespoon (15 ml) of olive oil in a large Dutch oven over medium heat. Working in batches, brown the beef on all sides. Set the browned beef aside.

Heat the remaining 1 tablespoon (15 ml) of olive oil in the same Dutch oven over medium heat. Sauté the shallots and garlic until translucent, about 1 minute.

Deglaze with ¼ cup (60 ml) of beef bone broth. Add the remaining broth and Dijon mustard.

Add the beef back to the Dutch oven and cook over low heat for 1 hour.

Step 3:

SUNNY PESTO-ROASTED VEGGIE BOWLS

2 russet potatoes, cut into ½-inch (1.3-cm) dice

2 cups (232 g) butternut squash, peeled and cut into ½-inch (1.3-cm) dice

1 red onion, cut into ½-inch (1.3-cm) dice

3 tbsp (45 ml) olive oil, divided

1 tsp salt

½ tsp black pepper

4 cups (364 g) broccoli, chopped into florets

While the beef Stroganoff is cooking, preheat the oven to 400°F (204°C). In a large bowl, toss together the potatoes, squash, red onion, 2 tablespoons (30 ml) of olive oil, salt and pepper. Spread the vegetables across a sheet pan and roast them in the oven for 20 minutes. Meanwhile, in the same bowl, toss the broccoli florets with the remaining 1 tablespoon (15 ml) of olive oil.

Step 4:

SILKY BEEF STROGANOFF

2 tbsp (30 g) unsalted ghee

2 lbs (907 g) cremini mushrooms, thinly sliced

Salt and pepper, to taste

While the vegetables are cooking, in a separate skillet, heat the ghee over medium heat, add the sliced mushrooms and sauté until golden brown and the liquid has evaporated, 5 to 7 minutes. Season with salt and pepper to taste. Set aside.

Step 5:

SUNNY PESTO-ROASTED VEGGIE BOWLS

After the vegetables have been roasting for 20 minutes, spread the broccoli on its own sheet pan and put it in the oven. Turn the vegetables that are already roasting. Roast all the vegetables for an additional 15 minutes until the potatoes and squash are tender and golden, the onion has begun to caramelize and the broccoli is starting to char. Remove everything from the oven and let it cool completely.

Step 6:

TUNA BURGERS WITH MAPLE-ROASTED CARROT SALAD

3 lbs (1.4 kg) tuna fillets, center cut, skin removed

1 tbsp (15 ml) coconut aminos

1 tbsp (15 ml) toasted sesame oil

2 shallots, minced

4 tsp (10 g) capers, drained and chopped

3 tsp (5 g) fresh ginger, finely grated on a microplane

2 tbsp (2 g) cilantro, finely chopped

½ tsp salt

¼ tsp black pepper

While the veggies are roasting, make the tuna burgers. Cut the tuna into ¼-inch (6-mm) chunks.

Place one-quarter of the cut tuna into a food processor and add the coconut aminos and sesame oil. Pulse into a paste.

Combine the pureed and chunky tuna in a bowl and add the minced shallots, capers, ginger, cilantro, salt and pepper.

(continued)

Shape this tuna burger mixture into eight patties.

Freeze four of the tuna patties for reheat night. Be sure to store them in an airtight container with parchment paper between the burgers, so they don't stick together.

Store the remaining four patties in an airtight container with parchment paper between the burgers and refrigerate over ice for cook night. *(Note: If it will be more than 1 day before you cook the tuna, store in the freezer.)*

Step 7:

FAST AND FRESH POKE BOWLS

PICKLED VEGGIES

1½ cups (360 ml) rice vinegar

2 tsp (10 g) coconut sugar

2 tsp (12 g) salt

3 cups (720 ml) warm water

1 (10-oz [283-g]) bag shredded carrots

2 cucumbers, sliced

1 (3-inch [7.5-cm]) piece ginger, sliced

After storing the tuna burgers, it's time to make the pickled veggies for the poke bowls. To pickle the vegetables, first make the sauce in a medium-sized storage container. Combine the rice vinegar, coconut sugar and salt. Slowly add the warm water and whisk until the sugar and salt are dissolved. Add the shredded carrots, cucumbers and ginger. Ensure that the vegetables are significantly covered in the liquid, and store in the refrigerator to pickle until ready to enjoy on cook night.

Step 8:

SESAME BEEF STIR-FRY WITH BOK CHOY

After finishing the pickled vegetables, return to the sesame beef stir-fry. If you used the Instant Pot to cook it, allow the Instant Pot to naturally release for 10 minutes, then manually release the vent and turn off the Instant Pot.

Allow the sesame beef to completely cool and then divide it into two equal portions. Pour each portion into an airtight container. Store one portion in the refrigerator for cook night and the other portion in the freezer for reheat night.

Step 9:

SILKY BEEF STROGANOFF

1½ cups (360 ml) coconut milk

Salt and pepper, to taste

After the beef for the Stroganoff has cooked for an hour, add the coconut milk and sautéed mushrooms to the beef in the Dutch oven. Stir until well combined and simmer for an additional 10 to 15 minutes to combine all the flavors and to let the sauce thicken. Season to taste with salt and pepper.

Remove the Dutch oven from the heat and allow the beef to cool completely. Divide the beef into two equal portions and place both portions in airtight containers. Store one portion in the refrigerator for cook night and the other portion in the freezer for reheat week.

FAST AND FRESH POKE BOWLS

Serves 4 on cook night and 4 on reheat night with the additional fresh ingredients found in the reheat grocery list on page 225

My sister is deathly allergic to seafood and I never ate it growing up, so I'll be honest and tell you this is a recipe Chaz influenced—and I'm glad he did, because it's amazing! He fell in love with poke bowls when we visited Hawaii, and when we came back, he asked if I could make it at home. What is poke, exactly? Poke means "to slice or cut" in Hawaiian and refers to cuts of raw, marinated fish. Since there's no cooking time, and thanks to the use of store-bought teriyaki sauce, this recipe comes together in a flash! Tip: While poke is typically served raw, there are instructions for how to cook the tuna if you (or your kids) would prefer it.

TUNA

1 lb (454 g) sushi-grade tuna, cut into bite-sized pieces

½ cup (120 ml) Paleo-friendly teriyaki sauce

SALAD AND TOPPINGS

5 oz (141 g) mixed greens

1 recipe pickled veggies from the weekly prep (page 213)

1 avocado, sliced

1 tbsp (9 g) sesame seeds

Radishes, sliced

PREP DAY:

See page 213 for the instructions to prep this recipe.

COOK NIGHT:

Chop the tuna into bite-sized pieces and coat the pieces with the teriyaki sauce. Marinate the tuna for as little as 15 minutes and as long as an hour. If you're nervous about eating raw fish, you can quickly sear the tuna steaks (do not cut them into bite-sized pieces) in a nonstick skillet or well-seasoned cast-iron skillet. Heat the pan over medium-high heat for 2 to 3 minutes. Add the tuna steaks and sear on each side for 2 to 3 minutes. Remove them from the pan and let rest for 2 to 4 minutes, then cut them into slices and pour the teriyaki sauce on top.

To serve, place the spring mix at the bottom of each bowl, top with the tuna poke and pickled vegetables and garnish with avocado slices, sesame seeds and fresh radish slices.

REHEAT NIGHT:

If your tuna is frozen, move it from the freezer to the refrigerator the night before making this dish to fully thaw. Also the night before, pickle another batch of vegetables using the instructions from prep day (page 213). On reheat night, follow all of the cook night instructions.

NOTE: If you'd prefer to make the sauce from scratch instead of using the teriyaki, see page 239 for the Poke Sauce recipe.

SUNNY PESTO-ROASTED VEGGIE BOWLS

Serves 4 on cook night and 4 on reheat night with the additional fresh ingredients found in the reheat grocery list on page 225

These sunny pesto veggie bowls are inspired by a restaurant I went to in college in Athens, Georgia. Chaz and I were both vegetarians in college, so the "make your own veggie bowl" was a great option for us. I always chose the same ingredients, the ones you'll find below. You can use this same concept to make a myriad of vegetarian bowls—simply swap out the veggies and the sauce to switch it up! You will be surprised how delicious Parmesan-free pesto can be, and while I love the store-bought version used here, my homemade version (on page 239) is even better if you have the time. I put it on everything! If you make it, you can put the homemade pesto into an ice cube tray and freeze individual cubes to use later.

½ recipe veggies from the weekly prep (page 211)

1 (6.5-oz [184-g]) container vegan pesto

1 cup (54 g) sun-dried tomatoes in oil, drained and roughly chopped

PREP DAY:

See page 211 for the prep ingredients and instructions.

COOK NIGHT:

Remove the vegetables and the pesto from the refrigerator.

Preheat the oven to 350°F (177°C) and line a sheet pan with parchment paper.

Spread the vegetables across the sheet pan and bake them in the oven for 5 to 7 minutes until they are warmed through.

Remove the pan from the oven and add the vegetables to a large serving bowl. Pour on the pesto and chopped sun-dried tomatoes and toss to coat.

REHEAT NIGHT:

To thaw the roasted veggies overnight, move them from the freezer to the refrigerator the night before reheat night. To thaw day of, move the container from the freezer to your countertop and allow the veggies to completely thaw at room temperature. For a quick thaw, submerge the container in room temperature water until completely thawed. Once thawed, follow the cook night instructions.

NOTE: If you'd prefer to make the pesto from scratch, see page 239 for the recipe.

SESAME BEEF STIR-FRY WITH BOK CHOY

Serves 4 on cook night and 4 on reheat night with the additional fresh ingredients found in the reheat grocery list on page 225

A friend of mine made this recipe having never once used sesame oil before, and it has changed her life! She now adds it to all of her stir-fries and Asian dishes—as do I! I adore the flavors in this dish and use this sauce for all different kinds of meats and vegetables. Bok choy is a type of Chinese cabbage, and it's a tasty way to switch up your veggies! Feel free to use chopped chicken to make sesame chicken! Just choose the "chicken" setting on your Instant Pot during prep day instead.

½ recipe sesame beef from the weekly prep (page 210)

1 tbsp (15 ml) toasted sesame oil

1 lb (454 g) bok choy, cut in half lengthwise and chopped into 1-inch (2.5-cm) pieces

1 clove garlic, minced

1 tbsp (15 ml) coconut aminos

Salt and pepper, to taste

1 tbsp (9 g) sesame seeds, for garnish (optional)

6 scallions, sliced, for serving (optional)

PREP DAY:

See page 210 for the instructions to prep this recipe.

COOK NIGHT:

Remove the sesame beef from the refrigerator and put it in a pot on the stovetop. Reheat the sesame beef over medium-low heat until warmed through, 8 to 10 minutes.

While the sesame beef is reheating, heat the sesame oil in a sauté pan over medium-high heat. Add the bok choy and sauté until it is tender. Add the garlic and sauté for 1 minute more, then add the coconut aminos and stir to combine. Season to taste with salt and pepper.

Serve the sesame beef over the sautéed bok choy with a garnish of sesame seeds and scallions, if desired.

REHEAT NIGHT:

To thaw the beef overnight, move it from the freezer to the refrigerator the night before reheat night, giving it adequate time to completely thaw. To thaw day of, move the container from the freezer to your countertop and allow the sesame beef to completely thaw at room temperature. For a quick thaw, submerge the container in room temperature water until completely thawed. Once thawed, follow the instructions for cook night.

NOTE: If you'd prefer to make the sesame-ginger sauce entirely from scratch, see page 239 for the recipe.

TUNA BURGERS WITH MAPLE-ROASTED CARROT SALAD

Serves 4 on cook night and 4 on reheat night with the additional fresh ingredients found in the reheat grocery list on page 225

I love this roasted carrot salad so much that it has officially joined my Thanksgiving menu. These tuna burgers are a great way to get kiddos to love seafood, and it's so nice that they freeze beautifully. You can pull them out of the freezer, let them thaw and have them ready in under ten minutes!

½ recipe tuna burgers from the weekly prep (page 211)

Light olive oil, for frying

MAPLE-ROASTED CARROTS

6 large carrots, unpeeled and sliced in half lengthwise and widthwise

2 tbsp (30 ml) olive oil

2 tbsp (30 ml) maple syrup

1 tsp salt

PREP DAY:

See page 211 for the prep ingredients and instructions.

COOK NIGHT:

If your tuna burgers are frozen, let them thaw fully before cooking. You can move them from the freezer to the refrigerator the night before cooking.

Preheat the oven to 400°F (204°C).

In a large bowl, toss together the carrots, olive oil, maple syrup and salt. Spread the carrots across a sheet pan and roast them in the oven for 25 minutes until they are tender and golden brown.

While the carrots are roasting, cook the tuna burgers. Heat the frying oil in a 12-inch (30-cm) nonstick skillet over medium-high heat and cook the patties for 3 to 4 minutes per side. Alternatively, you can cook the patties on a grill pan or grill. The internal temperature of the burger should be 165°F (74°C) on an instant-read thermometer.

Remove the carrots from the oven.

Serve the tuna patties with the roasted carrots.

REHEAT NIGHT:

Follow the instructions for cook night.

NOTE: If you'd like to serve these tuna burgers on buns, use my Paleo buns recipe on page 226.

SILKY BEEF STROGANOFF

Serves 4 on cook night and 4 on reheat night with the additional fresh ingredients found in the reheat grocery list on page 225

Beef Stroganoff is a luxurious dish that was created in Russia by a Frenchman, which explains the fusion of flavors. To be honest, mushrooms aren't even my favorite, and I *still* love this dish. The sauce is so creamy and bursting with umami flavor from the mushrooms. My kids eat three bowls each when I make this!

½ recipe beef Stroganoff from the weekly prep (page 210)

1 (9-oz [255-g]) box Cappello's fettuccine noodles

2 tbsp (30 g) unsalted ghee, melted

2 tbsp (8 g) parsley, chopped

PREP DAY:

See page 210 for the prep ingredients and instructions.

COOK NIGHT:

Remove the beef Stroganoff from the refrigerator and add it to a pot on the stovetop. Reheat it over medium heat until warmed through, 8 to 10 minutes.

While the beef is reheating, bring a large pot of water to a boil on the stovetop. Cook the pasta noodles according to the package directions.

Drain the pasta and return the noodles to the pot. Add the ghee and toss the noodles to coat.

Divide the noodles into servings, top with beef Stroganoff and garnish with chopped parsley.

REHEAT NIGHT:

To thaw the beef Stroganoff overnight, move it from the freezer to the refrigerator the night before reheat night. To thaw day of, move the container from the freezer to your countertop and allow the Stroganoff to completely thaw at room temperature. For a quick thaw, submerge the container in room temperature water until completely thawed. Once thawed, follow the cook night instructions.

WEEK 12 GROCERY LIST

PROTEIN
- ☐ 4 lbs (1.8 kg) sushi-grade tuna ● ●
- ☐ 4 lbs (1.8 kg) beef stew meat ● ●

PRODUCE
- ☐ 1 (4-inch [10-cm]) piece ginger ● ●
- ☐ 5 shallots ● ●
- ☐ 1 (10-oz [283-g]) bag shredded carrots ●
- ☐ 2 cucumbers ●
- ☐ 5 oz (141 g) mixed greens ●
- ☐ 1 avocado ●
- ☐ 1 bunch radishes ●
- ☐ 2 russet potatoes ●
- ☐ 2 cups (232 g) butternut squash ●
- ☐ 1 red onion ●
- ☐ 4 cups (364 g) broccoli ●
- ☐ 1 head garlic ● ●
- ☐ 1 lb (454 g) bok choy ●
- ☐ 1 bunch cilantro ●
- ☐ 6 large carrots ●
- ☐ 2 lbs (907 g) crimini mushrooms ●
- ☐ 1 bunch flat-leaf parsley ●
- ☐ 1 bunch scallions ●

SPICES
- ☐ Sesame seeds ● ●

PANTRY
- ☐ Coconut aminos ●
- ☐ Toasted sesame oil ● ●
- ☐ 1½ cups (360 ml) rice vinegar ●
- ☐ Coconut sugar ●
- ☐ 1 cup (54 g) sun-dried tomatoes ●
- ☐ Arrowroot ●
- ☐ 1 (32-oz [960-ml]) box beef bone broth ● ●
- ☐ Capers ●
- ☐ Maple syrup ●
- ☐ ¼ cup (60 ml) Dijon mustard ●
- ☐ 1 (13.5-oz [398-ml]) can coconut milk ●
- ☐ 1 (9-oz [255-g]) jar Paleo-friendly teriyaki sauce (I like Primal Kitchen No-Soy Island Teriyaki Sauce) ●
- ☐ 1 (8-oz [237-ml]) jar Paleo-friendly sesame-ginger sauce (I like Primal Kitchen Sesame Ginger Vinaigrette & Marinade) ●
- ☐ 1 (6.5-oz [184.2-g]) container vegan pesto (I like Gotham Greens Vegan Pesto) ●

DAIRY ALTERNATIVES
- ☐ Unsalted ghee (I like Fourth & Heart) ●

FREEZER
- ☐ 1 (9-oz [255-g]) box Paleo-friendly noodles (I like Cappello's Fettuccine Noodles) ●

RECIPES KEY: ● ● ● ● ●

Fast and Fresh Poke Bowls (page 214)
Sesame Beef Stir-Fry with Bok Choy (page 218)
Tuna Burgers with Maple-Roasted Carrot Salad (page 221)
Sunny Pesto-Roasted Veggie Bowls (page 217)
Silky Beef Stroganoff (page 222)

WEEK 12 REHEAT GROCERY LIST

FAST AND FRESH POKE BOWLS
- ☐ 1 lb (454 g) sushi-grade tuna
- ☐ 1 (9-oz [255-g]) jar Paleo-friendly teriyaki sauce (I like Primal Kitchen No-Soy Island Teriyaki Sauce)
- ☐ 1½ cups (360 ml) rice vinegar
- ☐ Coconut sugar
- ☐ 1 (10-oz [283-g]) bag shredded carrots
- ☐ 2 cucumbers
- ☐ 1 (3-inch [7.5-cm]) piece fresh ginger
- ☐ 1 avocado
- ☐ Sesame seeds
- ☐ 1 small bunch radishes
- ☐ 5 oz (141 g) mixed greens

SUNNY PESTO-ROASTED VEGGIE BOWLS
- ☐ 1 (6.5-oz [184-g]) container vegan pesto (I like Gotham Greens Vegan Pesto)
- ☐ 1 cup (54 g) sun-dried tomatoes

SESAME BEEF STIR-FRY WITH BOK CHOY
- ☐ 1 lb (454 g) bok choy
- ☐ Toasted sesame oil
- ☐ 1 clove garlic
- ☐ Coconut aminos
- ☐ 1 (8-oz [237-ml]) jar Paleo-friendly sesame-ginger sauce (I like Primal Kitchen Sesame Ginger Vinaigrette & Marinade)
- ☐ Sesame seeds
- ☐ 1 bunch scallions

TUNA BURGERS WITH MAPLE-ROASTED CARROT SALAD
- ☐ 6 large carrots
- ☐ Maple syrup

SILKY BEEF STROGANOFF
- ☐ 1 (9-oz [255-g]) box Paleo-friendly noodles (I like Cappello's Fettuccine Noodles)
- ☐ Unsalted ghee (I like Fourth & Heart)
- ☐ 1 bunch flat-leaf parsley

HOMEMADE SAUCES, DRESSINGS, SEASONINGS AND EXTRAS

We intentionally used lots of shortcuts and pre-made sauces throughout this cookbook to help you get dinner on the table as quickly as possible—but I can't recommend enough that you take some time to give these recipes a try! These homemade versions will absolutely knock your socks off. Enjoy!

TERIYAKI SAUCE (FOR PAGES 19 AND 181)

1 cup (240 ml) coconut aminos

½ cup (120 ml) fresh orange juice or pineapple juice

⅓ cup (80 ml) honey

4 tsp (20 g) fresh grated ginger

6 cloves garlic, pressed or minced

Pinch of red pepper flakes

2 tsp (5 g) arrowroot

In a small saucepan, combine the coconut aminos, orange juice, honey, ginger, garlic and red pepper flakes and bring to a simmer uncovered over medium heat. Whisk in the arrowroot to thicken. Let simmer, stirring occasionally, until the sauce reduces by half, about 7 minutes. Set aside to cool and store in an airtight container in the refrigerator.

PALEO BUNS (FOR PAGES 19, 164 AND 221)

(Makes 8 buns)

1½ cups (360 ml) warm water

1 (¼-oz [7-g]) packet yeast (about 2¼ tsp)

1 tbsp (15 ml) honey

3 tbsp (45 ml) olive oil

2 cups (250 g) cassava flour

½ cup (64 g) arrowroot

1 tbsp (14 g) xanthan gum

2 tbsp (16 g) coconut flour

1 tbsp (18 g) salt

Preheat your oven to 450°F (232°C) and line a sheet pan with parchment paper.

To make the dough, start by mixing the warm water, yeast and honey in a small bowl. Let the yeast activate until it's foamy, a full 5 minutes. Then, add the olive oil to the yeast mixture.

Using a stand mixer fitted with a dough hook, combine the cassava flour, arrowroot, xanthan gum, coconut flour and salt and mix.

Once the yeast mixture is foamy, slowly add it to the dry ingredients.

Knead this mixture on medium speed until the dough is fully incorporated and is no longer sticking to the sides of the bowl, 5 full minutes.

Roll the dough onto a lightly cassava-floured surface and, using a pastry cutter or a chef's knife, divide the dough into eight equal portions. Using your hands, roll each portion into a ball and place onto the sheet pan.

Bake in the oven for 12 to 14 minutes with an oven-safe bowl containing 1 cup (240 ml) of water on a rack below your sheet pan. This helps give the buns a "steamed" effect.

Store in an airtight container in the refrigerator for up to 2 days or in the freezer for up to 1 month.

ASIAN DRESSING

(FOR PAGE 19)

¼ cup (60 ml) olive oil

2 tsp (10 ml) sesame oil

3 tbsp (45 ml) rice vinegar

2 tbsp (30 ml) coconut aminos

2 tbsp (30 g) orange juice concentrate (the frozen kind)

2 tsp (3 g) fresh ginger, minced

¼ tsp garlic powder

In a small bowl, make the dressing by whisking together the olive oil, sesame oil, rice vinegar, coconut aminos, orange juice concentrate, grated ginger and garlic powder. Store in an airtight container in the refrigerator for 2 to 3 months.

THAI ALMOND SAUCE

(FOR PAGE 16)

1 (4-inch [10-cm]) piece ginger, roughly chopped

4 cloves garlic

1 cup (258 g) unsalted creamy almond butter (if you cannot find unsalted almond butter, omit the additional salt)

1 cup (240 ml) orange juice

½ cup (120 ml) coconut aminos

¼ cup (60 ml) honey

½ cup (120 ml) toasted sesame oil

1 tbsp (15 ml) Paleo-friendly sriracha

Salt, to taste

In a blender, combine the ginger, garlic, almond butter, orange juice, coconut aminos, honey, toasted sesame oil, sriracha and salt and blend until smooth.

When making this for your Prep, Cook, Freeze week, store half of the sauce in an airtight container in the refrigerator and the other half in the freezer. The sauce will keep for up to 2 months.

ALFREDO SAUCE

(FOR PAGES 23 AND 56)

3 cups (438 g) raw cashews

3 cups (720 ml) coconut milk

6 cloves garlic

2 tbsp (30 ml) lemon juice or vinegar

3 tbsp (15 g) nutritional yeast

⅓ cup (75 g) unsalted ghee

1½ tsp (9 g) salt

1½ tsp (9 g) black pepper

Make the Alfredo sauce by first soaking the cashews in hot water for 20 minutes. Drain the soaked cashews and put them in a blender with the coconut milk, garlic, lemon juice, nutritional yeast, ghee, salt and black pepper and blend until smooth. Store in an airtight container in the refrigerator for up to a week.

SWEET AND SOUR SAUCE

(FOR PAGE 20)

¾ to 1 cup (180 to 240 ml) pineapple juice (drained from a 20-oz [567-g] can pineapple chunks)

½ (20-oz [567-g]) can pineapple chunks

½ cup (120 ml) ketchup

½ cup (120 ml) coconut aminos

2 cloves garlic

1 (1-inch [2.5-cm]) piece fresh ginger, finely chopped or grated

1 tbsp (8 g) tapioca starch

Pinch of red pepper flakes

Blend all of the sauce ingredients in a high-powered blender. Store in an airtight container in the refrigerator. The sauce will keep for up to 2 months.

CHICKEN TIKKA MASALA

(FOR PAGE 24)

6 cloves garlic, minced

4 tsp (6 g) minced ginger

4 tsp (8 g) ground turmeric

2 tsp (4 g) garam masala

2 tsp (4 g) ground coriander

2 tsp (4 g) ground cumin

1 (13.5-oz [398-ml]) can coconut milk, divided

1 tbsp (18 g) kosher salt

2 lbs (907 g) boneless, skinless chicken breasts, cut into 1-inch (2.5-cm) dice

3 tbsp (42 g) ghee

1 small onion, chopped

1 (6-oz [170-g]) can tomato paste

¼ tsp ground cardamom

½ tsp crushed red pepper flakes

1 (15-oz [425-g]) can diced tomatoes

¾ cup (12 g) chopped fresh cilantro

Make your spice mixture by combining the minced garlic, ginger, turmeric, garam masala, coriander and cumin in a small bowl. Set aside.

Whisk one-half of the can of coconut milk together with the salt and half of the spice mixture in a medium bowl. Add this mixture to a storage container. Add the chicken and ensure it is fully submerged in the mixture. Cover and chill for 1 hour.

Heat the ghee in a large pot over medium heat. Add the onion, tomato paste, cardamom and red pepper flakes. Cook for about 5 minutes, stirring often, until the onion softens. Add the remaining half of the spice mixture and cook, continuing to stir, for about 4 minutes. Add the diced tomatoes with juices. Bring it all to a boil, then simmer, stirring often, until the sauce thickens, about 10 minutes.

Transfer the entire contents of the pot to a high-powered blender. Add the remaining coconut milk and the cilantro. Blend this mixture until smooth.

Return the sauce to the pot and add the chicken and remaining marinade. Coat the chicken in the sauce, and simmer, uncovered and undisturbed, until the chicken is fully cooked and the sauce has thickened, 20 to 30 minutes.

Once the chicken tikka masala has cooked, allow it to cool completely. Divide the chicken tikka masala into two equal portions. Store one portion in an airtight container in the refrigerator for cook night. Store the other half in an airtight container in the freezer for reheat night.

SPICE RUB (FOR PAGES 37, 164 AND 168)

1 tbsp (15 g) coconut sugar

1 tbsp (7 g) paprika

2 tsp (4 g) chili powder

1 tsp garlic powder

1 tsp onion powder

½ tsp ground cumin

1 tsp salt

½ tsp black pepper

Combine all the ingredients in a small bowl and whisk together. Store in an airtight container.

BARBECUE SAUCE

(FOR PAGES 37 AND 42)

1 cup (264 g) plus 2 tbsp (32 g) tomato paste

¾ cup (180 ml) apple cider vinegar

1½ cups (360 ml) water

1¾ cups (305 g) pitted dates

3 tbsp (47 g) mustard

1½ tbsp (23 ml) coconut aminos

1½ tsp (9 g) celery salt

3 cloves garlic, minced

1½ tsp (9 g) chili powder

1½ tsp (9 g) black pepper

½ tsp ground cloves

Make the barbecue sauce by combining all the ingredients in a blender and blending until smooth.

Store the sauce in an airtight container in the refrigerator for up to 2 months.

CILANTRO-LIME DRESSING

(FOR PAGE 38)

1 bunch cilantro

1 avocado

1 clove garlic

Juice from 1 lime

¼ cup (60 ml) olive oil

½ tsp salt

1 tbsp (15 ml) water (optional)

Make the dressing by combining all the ingredients in a food processor or blender and blending until smooth. You may add an additional 1 tablespoon (15 ml) of water, if desired, to thin out the dressing. Store in an airtight container in the refrigerator for up to 1 week.

GREEN CHILE SAUCE

(FOR PAGES 41 AND 77)

1 poblano pepper, halved and seeded

2 lbs (907 g) tomatillos, husks removed and sliced in half

4 cloves garlic, unpeeled and whole

1 jalapeño, halved lengthwise and seeded

2 tbsp (30 ml) olive oil, divided

Salt and pepper, to taste

2 yellow onions, halved and sliced

2 (4-oz [113-g]) cans green chiles, drained

½ cup (120 ml) lime juice

1 bunch cilantro

1 tbsp (6 g) cumin

(continued)

Preheat the oven to 400°F (204°C). Line a sheet pan with parchment paper and scatter the poblano, tomatillos, garlic and jalapeño on it. Drizzle with 1 tablespoon (15 ml) of olive oil and season to taste with salt and pepper. Roast the vegetables in the oven for 25 minutes until they are tender and starting to brown.

Remove the roasted vegetables from the oven and add to a blender. Add the onions, green chiles, lime juice, cilantro, cumin and remaining 1 tablespoon (15 ml) of olive oil. Blend until smooth.

When making this for your Prep, Cook, Freeze week, divide the sauce into two even portions. Put one portion in an airtight container in the refrigerator for cook night and the other half in an airtight container in the freezer for reheat week. This will keep in the refrigerator for up to 1 week and in the freezer for up to 2 months.

PIZZA DOUGH (FOR PAGE 42)

3 cups (720 ml) warm water

2 (¼-oz [7-g]) packets yeast (about 4½ tsp)

2 tbsp (30 ml) honey

6 tbsp (90 ml) olive oil

4 cups (500 g) cassava flour

1 cup (128 g) arrowroot

2 tbsp (16 g) xanthan gum

¼ cup (31 g) coconut flour

2 tbsp (36 g) kosher salt

For the pizza dough, start by mixing the warm water (between 110 and 115°F [43 and 46°C]), yeast and honey in the bowl of a stand mixer fitted with a dough hook. Let the yeast activate until it's foamy, about 5 minutes. Once the yeast begins to foam, add the olive oil.

In another large mixing bowl, combine the cassava flour, arrowroot, xanthan gum, coconut flour and salt.

Next, add the dry ingredients slowly to the foamy yeast mixture while the mixer is on its lowest setting. Knead this mixture in the stand mixture on medium speed until the dough is fully incorporated and is no longer sticking to the sides of the bowl.

Turn the dough out onto a lightly cassava-floured surface and divide the dough into two even portions. Form each portion into a disc and tightly wrap with plastic wrap. When making this for your Prep, Cook, Freeze week, store one disc in the refrigerator for cook night and the other dough disc in the freezer for reheat night.

To cook the dough: Preheat your oven to 450°F (232°C). Remove the pizza dough from the refrigerator, place it onto parchment paper and roll with a rolling pin until it is ¼ inch (6 mm) thick.

If you have a pizza stone, roll your dough into a circle. If you are going to use a traditional sheet pan, roll the dough into a rectangle. Either shape is perfectly fine. Use a fork to puncture the dough about halfway through to prevent pockets of bubbles. Start in the center and work your way out to about where the "crust" starts. Put your pizza crust in the oven for 15 minutes to precook, then add your toppings and bake for another 10 minutes.

ROMESCO SAUCE

(FOR PAGE 55)

2 (12-oz [340-g]) jars roasted red pepper, drained

1 cup (143 g) raw almonds

1½ cups (81 g) sun-dried tomatoes, including oil

2 cloves garlic

¼ cup (60 ml) red wine vinegar

2 tsp (2 g) smoked paprika

1 tsp salt

1 tsp cayenne

1 cup (240 ml) olive oil

¼ cup (15 g) fresh parsley

2 tbsp (30 ml) lemon juice

Combine all the ingredients in a blender and blend until smooth. Divide the sauce into two airtight containers, storing one in the refrigerator for cook night. Store the other sauce in the refrigerator or freezer for reheat night. It will keep in the refrigerator for 2 months or in the freezer for up to 6 months.

GREEK DRESSING

(FOR PAGES 59 AND 142)

1½ cups (360 ml) olive oil

¾ cup (180 ml) red wine vinegar

1 cup (240 ml) lemon juice

1 tbsp (4 g) fresh parsley (or 1 tsp dried parsley)

1 tbsp (4 g) fresh oregano (or 1 tsp dried oregano)

1 tbsp (8 g) minced garlic (about 4 cloves)

1 tbsp (18 g) salt

1 tsp black pepper

Make the dressing by combining all the ingredients in a dressing bottle and shaking until combined. Divide the sauce into two airtight containers, storing one in the refrigerator for cook night. Store the other in the refrigerator or freezer for reheat night. It will keep in the refrigerator for 2 months or in the freezer for up to 6 months.

PUMPKIN YELLOW CURRY SAUCE

(FOR PAGE 70)

2 tbsp (30 ml) olive oil

1 shallot, minced

1 (2-inch [5-cm]) piece fresh ginger, minced

4 cloves garlic, minced

3 tbsp (45 g) yellow curry paste

2 (13.5-oz [398-ml]) cans coconut milk

1 (15-oz [425-g]) can pumpkin puree

In a large pot, heat the olive oil over medium-high heat. Add the shallot, ginger and garlic and sauté until the shallot is translucent, about 3 minutes.

Add the curry paste and stir frequently for 1 minute. Add the coconut milk and stir until combined. Add the pumpkin puree and stir until combined.

Store in an airtight container in the refrigerator for up to a week.

TACO SEASONING

(FOR PAGE 73)

1 tbsp (6 g) chili powder

1½ tsp (3 g) ground cumin

1 tsp salt

1 tsp black pepper

½ tsp garlic powder

½ tsp onion powder

½ tsp paprika

¼ tsp red pepper flakes

¼ tsp dried oregano

1 tsp coconut or almond flour

Combine all the ingredients in a small bowl and whisk together. Store in an airtight container.

PORK FOR POZOLE AND TACOS AL PASTOR

(FOR PAGES 73 AND 77)

4 lbs (1.8 kg) pork shoulder

Salt and pepper

2 tbsp (30 ml) olive oil

1 large yellow onion, diced

6 cloves garlic, minced

1 lb (454 g) tomatillos, husked and cut into quarters

(continued)

2 jalapeños or serrano peppers, seeded and chopped

1 poblano pepper, chopped

2 bay leaves

1 tbsp (3 g) dried Mexican oregano (or regular dried oregano)

6 cups (1.4 L) chicken bone broth

Start by setting the Instant Pot to sauté. Season the pork with salt and pepper. Add the pork to the Instant Pot and sear on all sides (you can cut the pork into chunks if necessary to fit into the Instant Pot).

Remove the pork from the Instant Pot and set aside.

Pour the olive oil into the Instant Pot and sauté the onion until translucent. Add the garlic and sauté until fragrant, about 1 minute. Add the tomatillos and sauté for 5 more minutes until the tomatillos start to soften.

Add the chopped jalapeños and poblano pepper, bay leaves and oregano. Stir to combine and turn off the Instant Pot. Return the pork to the Instant Pot and pour in the chicken bone broth. Cover and set the Instant Pot to Stew for 1 hour.

Discard the bay leaves before serving.

TACOS AL PASTOR SAUCE

(FOR PAGE 73)

3 cloves garlic

1 tsp dried oregano

½ tsp ground cumin

1 guajillo chile

½ to 1 arbol chile or ¼ tsp chile de arbol powder (optional)

¼ tsp paprika

3 tbsp (48 g) tomato paste

¼ cup (60 ml) distilled white vinegar

5 dates or ¼ cup (50 g) coconut sugar

½ cup (83 g) pineapple tidbits or chunks with juice

½ cup (120 ml) orange juice

¼ cup (60 ml) lime juice

1 tsp salt

Make the sauce by combining all the ingredients in a blender. Blend until smooth. Divide the sauce into two even portions and put each portion in an airtight container. Store one portion in the refrigerator for up to a week for cook night and the other portion in the freezer for reheat week.

TARTAR SAUCE

(FOR PAGE 95)

½ cup (120 ml) Paleo-friendly mayonnaise

½ cup (120 ml) unsweetened plain Paleo-friendly yogurt

2 tbsp (20 g) shallot, minced

2 tbsp (30 g) cornichons, finely chopped

1 tbsp (15 ml) lemon juice

2 tsp (5 g) capers, finely chopped

Salt and pepper, to taste

Make the sauce by combining all the ingredients in a bowl and stirring to combine. Store in an airtight container in the refrigerator for up to 2 weeks.

CAESAR DRESSING

(FOR PAGE 91)

½ cup (120 ml) Paleo-friendly mayonnaise

1 tsp minced anchovies

1 clove garlic, minced

1 tsp white wine vinegar

1 tsp whole grain mustard

1 tbsp (15 ml) lemon juice

½ tsp salt

½ tsp black pepper

To make the dressing, combine all the ingredients in a bowl and whisk until thoroughly combined. Store it in an airtight container in the refrigerator for up to 7 days.

BUFFALO SAUCE

(FOR PAGE 96)

½ cup (120 ml) hot sauce
2 tbsp (30 ml) honey
2 tsp (2 g) paprika
1 tsp garlic salt
¼ cup (60 ml) olive oil

To make the sauce, combine all the ingredients in a bowl and whisk until thoroughly combined. Store it in an airtight container in the refrigerator for up to a week.

RANCH DRESSING

(FOR PAGE 96)

½ cup (120 ml) unsweetened plain Paleo-friendly yogurt
½ cup (120 ml) Paleo-friendly mayonnaise
1 tsp dried dill
½ tsp dried parsley
½ tsp dried chives
¼ tsp onion powder
½ tsp garlic powder
¼ tsp fine sea salt
¼ tsp black pepper

To make the dressing, combine all the ingredients in a bowl and whisk until thoroughly combined. Store it in an airtight container in the refrigerator for 5 to 7 days.

CREAMY JALAPEÑO SAUCE

(FOR PAGE 110)

½ cup (120 ml) Paleo-friendly sour cream or unsweetened plain yogurt
½ cup (120 ml) Paleo-friendly mayonnaise
1 tsp dried dill
½ tsp dried parsley
½ tsp dried chives
¼ tsp onion powder
½ tsp garlic powder
¼ tsp fine sea salt
¼ tsp black pepper
½ cup (8 g) cilantro
2 fresh jalapeños, seeded
2 tbsp (30 ml) fresh lime juice

In a blender, combine the sour cream, mayonnaise, dill, parsley, chives, onion powder, garlic powder, salt, pepper, cilantro, jalapeños and lime juice. Blend until smooth.

Store in an airtight container in the refrigerator for up to a week.

PICO DE GALLO

(FOR PAGE 106)

4 Roma tomatoes, ¼-inch (6-mm) dice
½ white onion, ¼-inch (6-mm) dice
¼ cup (4 g) chopped cilantro
1 tsp lime juice
¼ tsp salt
¼ tsp black pepper

Make the pico de gallo in a large bowl by combining the tomatoes, white onion, cilantro, lime juice, salt and pepper. Stir to mix and store in an airtight container in the refrigerator for 2 to 3 days.

GUACAMOLE (FOR PAGE 106)

2 ripe avocados, roughly mashed
½ white onion, ¼-inch (6-mm) dice
¼ cup (4 g) chopped cilantro
1 jalapeño, seeded and minced
Juice from 1 lime
Salt and pepper, to taste

Make the guacamole in a large bowl by combining the avocados, onion, cilantro, jalapeño and lime juice, then seasoning to taste with salt and pepper. Store in an airtight container in the refrigerator for 2 to 3 days.

WAFFLES (FOR PAGE 113)

6 eggs
2 tbsp (30 ml) vanilla
¾ cup (170 g) unsalted ghee, melted
3 tbsp (45 ml) lemon juice
3 tbsp (45 ml) honey
2¼ cups (540 ml) coconut milk
3 cups (375 g) cassava flour
⅔ cup (63 g) almond flour
⅔ cup (83 g) coconut flour
⅔ cup (85 g) tapioca starch (arrowroot works great, too)
1½ tsp (7 g) baking soda
1½ tsp (9 g) salt

Make the waffles in a large bowl by combining the eggs, vanilla, melted ghee, lemon juice, honey and coconut milk. Whisk to thoroughly combine.

In a different bowl, combine all the dry ingredients and whisk together. Add the dry ingredients to the wet ingredients and gently fold together.

Set a waffle iron to a medium-high setting and generously spray with avocado oil cooking spray. Pour about ½ cup (120 ml) of batter onto the waffle iron and cook until your waffle iron says it is done—about 2 minutes. Remove the waffle and set aside to cool.

You should get eight regular-sized waffles. Wrap all the waffles (in two batches of four) in parchment paper and store in an airtight container in the freezer for both cook and reheat night. These waffles will keep in the freezer for about a month.

FAJITA SEASONING

(FOR PAGE 127)

2 tbsp (15 g) chili powder
1 tbsp (6 g) cumin
1 tbsp (7 g) paprika
1 tbsp (7 g) garlic powder
1½ tsp (4 g) onion powder
Pinch of cayenne pepper
¾ tsp salt
¾ tsp black pepper

Combine all the ingredients in a small bowl and whisk to combine. Store in an airtight container.

SUN-DRIED TOMATO BRUSCHETTA (FOR PAGE 128)

½ cup (27 g) sun-dried tomatoes with oil, sliced
2 tsp (12 g) kosher salt
2 cloves garlic, minced
2 beefsteak tomatoes, diced
⅓ cup (13 g) basil leaves, sliced

Combine all the ingredients in a large mixing bowl. Store in an airtight container in the refrigerator for up to 5 days.

DIABLO SAUCE

(FOR PAGE 131)

2 tbsp (30 ml) olive oil

½ cup (80 g) red onion, diced

½ cup (80 g) yellow onion, diced

1 red bell pepper, seeded and diced

2 cloves garlic, minced

1 tbsp (16 g) tomato paste

⅓ cup (80 ml) chicken bone broth

1 (15-oz [425-g]) can diced tomatoes with their juice

1 arbol chile or ¼ tsp chile de árbol powder

1 guajillo chile

½ tsp dried oregano

½ tsp salt

½ tsp black pepper

Heat the olive oil in a large skillet over medium heat. Add the red and yellow onion, as well as the red bell pepper. Sauté until the onions are translucent and the red bell pepper is tender, 3 to 5 minutes. Add the garlic and tomato paste and sauté until fragrant, about 1 minute more.

Deglaze the skillet with the chicken bone broth.

Add the diced tomatoes with juice, arbol and guajillo chiles, oregano, salt and black pepper and stir to combine.

Simmer uncovered for 10 minutes until the sauce thickens a bit.

Pour the sauce into a blender and blend until smooth.

Allow the sauce to cool and divide it into two equal portions. Place each portion in an airtight container. Put one portion in the refrigerator for cook night and the other portion in the freezer for reheat night.

EGGPLANT TORTILLAS

(FOR PAGE 142)

2 medium eggplants

Salt

Olive oil

Line two sheet pans with parchment paper. Slice the eggplant into ¼-inch (6-mm)-thick circles and line them up in the sheet pans. Sprinkle the eggplant with salt and let the eggplants "sweat" for 30 minutes. Meanwhile, preheat the oven to 375°F (191°C).

Once the eggplants are done "sweating," gently dry them with paper towels, then brush the slices with olive oil on both sides. Bake them in the oven for 10 minutes, then flip them over and bake for another 10 minutes.

Remove the eggplants from the oven and let cool. Divide them into two equal portions, then wrap each portion in between sheets of parchment paper and place them in a resealable bag. Store one bag in the refrigerator for cook night and the other bag in the freezer for reheat night.

HONEY MUSTARD DRESSING

(FOR PAGE 145)

1 tbsp (15 g) tahini

1 tbsp (15 ml) Dijon mustard

1 tbsp (15 ml) grainy mustard

1 tbsp (15 ml) honey

2 tbsp (30 ml) lemon juice

¼ cup (60 ml) olive oil

1 bunch parsley leaves, roughly chopped

Salt and pepper, to taste

(continued)

Put all the ingredients in a medium bowl and whisk to combine. Adjust the seasoning with additional salt and pepper. Store in an airtight container in the refrigerator for up to 10 days.

ROPA VIEJA STEAK IN HOMEMADE SAUCE

(FOR PAGE 146)

2 lbs (907 g) flank steak

Salt and pepper

¼ cup (60 ml) olive oil

1 onion, thinly sliced

1 red bell pepper, seeded and thinly sliced

6 cloves garlic, minced

1 tbsp (7 g) sweet paprika (or 1 tsp smoked paprika)

2 tsp (2 g) dried oregano

2 tsp (2 g) cumin

¼ tsp cayenne pepper

1 (6-oz [170-g]) can tomato paste

1 (28-oz [794-g]) can diced tomatoes

2 bay leaves

1 tbsp (18 g) kosher salt

2 tbsp (30 ml) white wine vinegar

¼ cup (45 g) capers, drained

Season the flank steak with salt and pepper and cut it into pieces that will fit inside an Instant Pot. Set an Instant Pot to the sauté setting and, working in batches, brown the flank steak on both sides. Remove from the Instant Pot and set aside. Keep the Instant Pot on the sauté setting and pour in the olive oil. Once the oil is hot, add the onion and bell pepper and sauté until soft, 3 to 5 minutes.

Add the garlic and sauté until fragrant, about 1 more minute. Add the spices and tomato paste and sauté until fragrant. Turn off the Instant Pot and return the flank steak to the pot. Add the diced tomatoes, bay leaves, salt, vinegar and capers.

Set to the Meat/Stew setting for 90 minutes, and let the Instant Pot naturally release when the cooking is complete.

THAI BASIL BEEF IN HOMEMADE SAUCE

(FOR PAGE 150)

2 tbsp (30 ml) olive oil

2 lbs (907 g) flank steak

Salt and pepper

1 yellow onion, thinly sliced

2 medium carrots, julienned or coarsely grated

1 red bell pepper, julienned

5 cloves garlic, thinly sliced

½ cup (120 ml) chicken bone broth

2 tbsp (30 ml) coconut aminos

1 tbsp (15 ml) fish sauce

1 tsp coconut sugar

In a large skillet or wok, heat the olive oil over high heat. Season the flank steak with salt and pepper and sear the beef, 2 to 3 minutes. Remove the beef from the pan and set aside. Put the onion and carrots in the same pan and cook for 5 minutes, until the vegetables are tender. Add the red bell pepper and garlic and cook for 1 minute more.

Add the chicken bone broth, coconut aminos, fish sauce and coconut sugar and stir to combine. Return the beef to the pan and cook over medium heat until the beef is completely cooked through and the sauce has thickened, 5 to 7 minutes. Let the mixture cool, then store half in an airtight container in the refrigerator for cook night and half in the freezer for reheat night.

CAROLINA VINEGAR SAUCE

(FOR PAGE 164)

1 cup (240 ml) apple cider vinegar
2 tbsp (30 ml) lemon juice
2 tbsp (30 ml) coconut aminos
2 tbsp (30 ml) honey
2 tbsp (30 g) coconut sugar
1 tsp cayenne pepper
1 tsp salt
1 tsp black pepper

Combine all of the ingredients in a saucepan over low heat. Stir continually until all of the ingredients are combined. Remove from the heat and cool completely. Store in a jar or a bottle with a lid. This barbecue sauce can last up to 2 months in the refrigerator.

JERK SEASONING

(FOR PAGE 178)

1 tbsp (7 g) garlic powder
1 tbsp (7 g) onion powder
2 tsp (2 g) cayenne pepper
1 tsp dried thyme
1 tsp dried parsley
1 tbsp (15 g) coconut sugar
2 tsp (12 g) salt
½ tsp black pepper
½ tsp red pepper flakes
½ tsp ground nutmeg
½ tsp ground cinnamon
¼ tsp cumin
¼ tsp cloves

Combine all the ingredients in a small bowl and whisk together. Store in an airtight container.

MANGO-PINEAPPLE SALSA

(FOR PAGE 178)

1 mango, diced
1 cup (165 g) pineapple, diced
½ small red onion, ¼-inch (6-mm) dice
1 red bell pepper, ¼-inch (6-mm) dice
¼ cup (4 g) chopped cilantro
1 tbsp (15 ml) lime juice

Combine all the salsa ingredients in a bowl and stir to combine. Store in an airtight container in the refrigerator for 2 to 3 days.

ENCHILADA SAUCE

(FOR PAGE 186)

6 tbsp (90 ml) olive oil or ghee
6 tbsp (48 g) arrowroot
6 tbsp (45 g) chili powder
4 tsp (8 g) ground cumin
2 tsp (4 g) garlic powder
2 tsp (4 g) onion powder
2 tsp (12 g) salt, plus more to taste
2 (6-oz [170-g]) cans tomato paste
4 cups (960 ml) chicken bone broth
Black pepper, to taste

Heat the oil or ghee in a medium saucepan over high heat.

Once the ghee is hot, add the arrowroot, chili powder, cumin, garlic powder, onion powder and salt. Whisk constantly until the spices become fragrant, 1 to 2 minutes. Whisk in the tomato paste and then slowly add the chicken bone broth.

(continued)

Bring the mixture to a boil, then reduce to a low simmer and cook, whisking frequently, until the sauce begins to thicken, 5 to 7 minutes.

Remove the enchilada sauce from the heat and add more salt and pepper to taste (if needed). Set aside to cool. Store in an airtight container in the refrigerator for 2 to 3 months.

CAULIFLOWER HUMMUS

(FOR PAGE 196)

1½ cups (150 g) cauliflower, cut into large florets

¼ cup (60 ml) lemon juice

¼ cup (65 g) tahini

1 clove garlic

1 tbsp (15 ml) olive oil

½ tsp ground cumin

½ tsp salt

Steam the cauliflower florets using a steamer basket or, if you don't have one, place a colander inside a large pot and add 1 cup (240 ml) of water to the pot. Bring the water to a boil, put the chopped cauliflower in the colander, cover and steam for 3 to 5 minutes, until the cauliflower is fork-tender. Set aside to cool.

Put the lemon juice and tahini in a food processor and process until the mixture is whipped and light in color. Add the steamed cauliflower, garlic, olive oil, cumin and salt and blend until smooth. Store in an airtight container in the refrigerator for 2 to 3 days until cook night.

POMEGRANATE LAMB COOKED IN HOMEMADE SAUCE (FOR PAGE 203)

2 tbsp (30 ml) olive oil

2 lbs (907 g) lamb stew meat

2 tsp (12 g) salt

1 tsp black pepper

1 yellow onion, diced

2 cloves garlic, minced

1 tsp allspice

1 tsp harissa spice

3 cups (720 ml) pomegranate juice

2 tbsp (30 ml) balsamic vinegar

1 tbsp (6 g) fresh mint leaves, chopped

Preheat your oven to 300°F (149°C). Adjust your oven racks to accommodate the Dutch oven for the lamb.

In the Dutch oven, heat the olive oil over medium-high heat. Season the lamb with salt and pepper and then add the lamb (in batches if necessary, so as not to crowd the pan) and brown the meat. Remove the lamb from the pot and set aside.

Add the onion to the same pot and sauté until translucent, 3 to 5 minutes. Add the garlic, allspice and harissa and sauté until fragrant, about 1 minute more. Add the pomegranate juice, balsamic vinegar and chopped mint and stir to combine.

Return the lamb to the pot and cover with the lid. Place in the oven and cook for 2 hours, or until the lamb is fork-tender.

FIG BALSAMIC GLAZE

(FOR PAGE 204)

1 cup (240 ml) white grape juice
4 dried figs
⅓ cup (80 ml) balsamic vinegar
¼ tsp kosher salt

Make the fig balsamic sauce by combining all the ingredients in a high-powered blender. Start the blender and increase the speed slowly to high. Blend on high until all ingredients are fully combined and warmed, about 2 minutes.

Store in an airtight container in the refrigerator for 2 to 3 months.

POKE SAUCE (FOR PAGE 214)

1 cup (240 ml) coconut aminos
¼ cup (60 ml) sesame oil
1 (2-inch [5-cm]) piece ginger, finely grated
2 bunches scallions, white and green parts separated, sliced
¼ cup (60 ml) honey
½ cup (120 ml) orange juice
4 shallots, finely minced
4 tsp (20 g) chile-garlic paste

Make the sauce by combining the coconut aminos, sesame oil, ginger, white parts of the scallions, honey, orange juice, shallots and chile-garlic paste. Reserve the green parts of the scallions for garnishing. Divide the poke sauce in half, storing half in an airtight container in the refrigerator for up to a week and a half in an airtight container in the freezer.

PESTO (FOR PAGE 217)

6 cups (144 g) fresh basil
4 cloves garlic
1 cup (240 ml) olive oil
½ cup (68 g) pine nuts
2 tsp (12 g) salt
2 tsp (10 ml) lemon juice
1 tsp nutritional yeast

Make the pesto by combining all the ingredients in a food processor or blender and blending until smooth. Divide the pesto into two equal portions. Keep both portions in airtight containers. Place one container in the refrigerator (for 2 to 3 days) for cook night and the other one in the freezer (for 1 to 2 months) for reheat night.

SESAME-GINGER SAUCE

(FOR PAGE 218)

1 bunch scallions, sliced, green and white parts divided
3 cloves garlic, minced
1 (1-inch [2.5-cm]) piece fresh ginger, minced
2 tbsp (30 g) coconut sugar
¼ cup (60 ml) coconut aminos
1 tsp rice vinegar
1 tbsp (15 ml) toasted sesame oil
2 tsp (10 ml) sriracha (optional, for heat)

In a small bowl, combine the white parts of the scallions (reserve the green parts for garnishing), garlic, ginger, coconut sugar, coconut aminos, rice vinegar, sesame oil and sriracha (if using). Whisk to combine. Store in an airtight container in the refrigerator for 2 to 3 months.

PALEO PANTRY AND SUBSTITUTIONS

SPICES

BARBECUE
☐ Primal Palate Barbecue Rub

TACO SEASONING
☐ Primal Palate Taco Seasoning
☐ Siete Taco Seasoning

FAJITA SEASONING
☐ Balanced Bites Taco & Fajita Spice Blend

HARISSA SEASONING
☐ Frontier Co-Op Organic Harissa Seasoning

JERK SEASONING
☐ Primal Palate Jerk Seasoning
☐ Frontier Co-Op Jamaica Jerk Seasoning

PALEO BREAD CRUMBS

☐ Jeff Nathan Creations Chef Gourmet Panko Plain Gluten Free
☐ Paleo Powder Seasoned Coating Mix

DRESSINGS AND MARINADES

GREEK
☐ Primal Kitchen Greek Vinaigrette & Marinade

RANCH
☐ Primal Kitchen Ranch Dressing
☐ Tessemae's Classic Ranch
☐ Noble Made Classic Ranch Dressing & Marinade
☐ Whole30 House Ranch Dressing and Dip
☐ Sir Kensington's Classic Ranch
☐ Tessemae's Organic Habanero Ranch Dressing

CILANTRO-LIME DRESSING
☐ Tessemae's Cilantro Lime Ranch Dressing & Dip
☐ Primal Kitchen Cilantro Lime Dressing & Marinade

CAESAR
☐ Primal Kitchen Caesar Dressing & Marinade
☐ Tessemae's Organic Creamy Caesar Dressing
☐ Thrive Market Caesar Dressing & Marinade

HONEY MUSTARD DRESSING
☐ Primal Kitchen Honey Mustard Dressing & Marinade
☐ Tessemae's Organic Honey Mustard
☐ Thrive Market Honey Mustard Dressing & Marinade

FIG BALSAMIC GLAZE
☐ Sur La Table Fig Balsamic Glaze

PESTO
☐ Gotham Greens Vegan Pesto
☐ Le Grand Garden Pesto

SESAME-GINGER DRESSING
☐ Primal Kitchen Sesame Ginger Vinaigrette & Marinade

CONDIMENTS

TARTAR SAUCE
- ☐ Primal Kitchen Tartar Sauce

KETCHUP
- ☐ Primal Kitchen Ketchup
- ☐ Tessemae's Organic Ketchup
- ☐ Noble Made Tomato Ketchup
- ☐ Good Food for Good Ketchup

MAYONNAISE
- ☐ Primal Kitchen Vegan Mayo
- ☐ Tessemae's Organic Mayonnaise
- ☐ Chosen Foods Classic Mayo

SAUCES AND SALSAS

BARBECUE SAUCE
- ☐ Primal Kitchen Classic BBQ Sauce
- ☐ Tessemae's Matty's Organic BBQ Sauce
- ☐ Noble Made Classic BBQ Sauce
- ☐ Good Food for Good Classic BBQ Sauce
- ☐ Kevin's Paleo BBQ Sauce—Original
- ☐ Noble Made Mustard BBQ Sauce
- ☐ Primal Kitchen Hawaiian Style BBQ Sauce

GREEN CHILE SAUCE
- ☐ Double Take Salsa Co. Verde Good Green Chile Salsa
- ☐ Siete Green Enchilada Sauce
- ☐ Fody Verde Saucy Enchilada Sauce
- ☐ Sprouts Organic Green Chile Enchilada Sauce
- ☐ Siete Red Enchilada Sauce

MANGO SALSA
- ☐ Stonewall Kitchen Mango Lime Salsa

ROMESCO SAUCE
- ☐ Chosen Foods Spanish Romesco Simmer Sauce
- ☐ Romesco Sauce by Espinaler
- ☐ Matiz Catalan Romesco Sauce

ALFREDO SAUCE
- ☐ Primal Kitchen No-Dairy Garlic Alfredo Sauce
- ☐ Primal Kitchen No-Dairy Alfredo Sauce

MARINARA AND TOMATO SAUCE
- ☐ Primal Kitchen Tomato Basil Marinara Sauce
- ☐ Thrive Market Organic Marinara Tomato Sauce
- ☐ Organico Bello Marinara Organic Pasta Sauce
- ☐ Muir Glen Classic Marinara, No Sugar Added, Pasta Sauce
- ☐ Lucini Italia Organic Rustic Tomato Basil Sauce

CURRY SAUCE
- ☐ Yai's Thai Yellow Thai Coconut Curry

THAI ALMOND SAUCE
- ☐ Yai's Thai Almond Sauce

AL PASTOR SAUCE
- ☐ Good Food for Good Mild Taco Sauce

BUFFALO SAUCE
- ☐ Primal Kitchen Buffalo Sauce
- ☐ Tessemae's Buffalo Sauce
- ☐ Noble Made Buffalo Sauce (Mild, Medium or Hot)
- ☐ Whole30 Buffalo Vinaigrette Dressing & Marinade

BRUSCHETTA
- ☐ DeLallo Sun-Dried Tomato Bruschetta
- ☐ Stonewall Kitchen Tomato Herb Bruschetta Spread

LATIN SIMMER SAUCE FOR THE SMOKY ROPA VIEJA (PAGE 146)
- ☐ Mesa de Vida Smoky Latin Cooking & Seasoning Sauce

THAI COCONUT SAUCE FOR THE THAI BASIL BEEF (PAGE 150)

- ☐ Kevin's Thai Coconut Sauce

HARISSA

- ☐ Mina Harissa Sauce
- ☐ Haven's Kitchen Zippy Chili Harissa Sauce

TERIYAKI SAUCE

- ☐ Primal Kitchen No-Soy Teriyaki Sauce & Marinade
- ☐ Kevin's Paleo-Keto Teriyaki Sauce
- ☐ Coconut Secret Soy-Free Teriyaki Sauce
- ☐ Noble Made Classic Marinade & Cooking Sauce
- ☐ Primal Kitchen No-Soy Island Teriyaki Sauce

MUHAMMARA SAUCE FOR THE POMEGRANATE LAMB (PAGE 203)

- ☐ Chosen Foods Muhammara Red Pepper Simmer Sauce

TIKKA MASALA SAUCE

- ☐ Good Food for Good Tikka Masala Cooking Sauce
- ☐ Nummy Nibbles Tikka Masala Cooking Sauce
- ☐ Kevin's Tikka Masala Sauce

HOT SAUCE

- ☐ Yai's Thai Chili Garlic Hot Sauce
- ☐ Yellowbird Organic Sriracha

COCONUT AMINOS

- ☐ Big Tree Farms Original Organic Coconut Aminos
- ☐ Thrive Market Organic Coconut Aminos
- ☐ Noble Made by The New Primal Original Coconut Aminos

FISH SAUCE

- ☐ Red Boat Fish Sauce

DOUGHS AND BATTERS

PIZZA CRUSTS

- ☐ Cappello's Naked Pizza Crust
- ☐ Mikey's Grain-Free Pizza Crust
- ☐ Liberated Paleo Pizza Crust
- ☐ Simple Mills Almond Flour Pizza Dough Mix

PANCAKE AND WAFFLE MIXES

- ☐ Birch Benders Paleo Pancake & Waffle Mix
- ☐ Bob's Red Mill Paleo Pancake & Waffle Mix
- ☐ Simple Mills Almond Flour Pancake & Waffle Mix
- ☐ Purely Elizabeth Grain-Free Pancake Mix
- ☐ Julian Bakery Paleo Thin Pancake & Waffle Mix

ENGLISH MUFFINS/BUNS

- ☐ Mikey's Grain-Free English Muffins, 4 pack

PASTAS

- ☐ Cappello's Grain Free Pastas
- ☐ Jovial Grain Free Cassava Pastas

HUMMUS

- ☐ Lilly's Organic Original Keto-Cauliflower Hummus
- ☐ Naya Cauliflower Hummus

DAIRY ALTERNATIVES

COCONUT MILK (USE FULL-FAT, UNSWEETENED CANNED COCONUT MILK)

- ☐ Thrive Market Organic Coconut Milk, Regular
- ☐ Native Forest Organic Coconut Milk, Simple
- ☐ Sprouts Organic Coconut Milk
- ☐ Thai Kitchen Organic Coconut Milk, Unsweetened

COCONUT CREAM

- ☐ Thrive Market Organic Coconut Cream, Extra Thick
- ☐ Thai Kitchen Coconut Cream, Unsweetened
- ☐ Sprouts Organic Coconut Cream

SOUR CREAM

- ☐ Forager Project Organic Dairy-Free Sour Cream

RICOTTA

- ☐ Kite Hill Ricotta

YOGURT

- ☐ Kite Hill Plain Unsweetened Greek Style Yogurt
- ☐ Lavva Original Plant-Based Yogurt
- ☐ GT's CocoYo Pure Living Coconut Yogurt
- ☐ Forager Project Unsweetened Plain Cashewmilk Yogurt

FETA CHEESE

- ☐ Violife Vegan Feta

MOZZARELLA CHEESE

- ☐ Miyoko's Fresh Vegan Mozzarella

PALEO-FRIENDLY PROTEINS

BACON

- ☐ Applegate Natural No Sugar Uncured Bacon
- ☐ Garrett Valley Sugar Free Turkey Bacon
- ☐ Pederson's Natural Farms Bacon, Uncured, No Sugar, Smoked

CHORIZO

- ☐ Pederson's Natural Farms Chorizo, No Sugar Added
- ☐ Mulay's Chorizo Ground Sausage

BONE BROTHS

BEEF

- ☐ Kettle & Fire Classic Beef Bone Broth
- ☐ Thrive Market Grass-Fed Beef Bone Broth
- ☐ Bare Bones Classic Beef Bone Broth

CHICKEN

- ☐ Kettle & Fire Classic Chicken Bone Broth
- ☐ Thrive Market Organic Chicken Bone Broth
- ☐ Bare Bones Chicken Bone Broth

ACKNOWLEDGMENTS

First, to God, for giving me a life that is so wildly above and beyond my wildest dreams. Thank you for giving me Chaz, Ella and Owen. Thank you for orchestrating this cookbook and every other opportunity in my life. I am so blessed by the purpose you've entrusted me with.

To Chaz, I never expected to love someone so much. You fiercely support me in every single entrepreneurial venture I start. You finish all of my "in process" recipes when no one else will. You pray for me, lead me, encourage me and challenge me. You are the most steadfast human being I've ever met. You believe in me even when I don't believe in myself.

To my precious kiddos, *you* are the reason this cookbook exists. Ella, we will never stop thanking God that you were born. He placed you in our lives in His perfect timing. Prioritizing your precious little being when you were out of the hospital but could have still been in my body felt like a "career setback" at the time. Turns out you catapulted me into the perfect career. You are the reason I started Olive You Whole, and I can never thank you enough. Ella, you are somehow more outgoing than I am. You wake up every morning with a passion to change the world. Your eyes and smile have more joy than sunshine on a summer's day. We know your love and your creative soul will impact so many lives. We're so proud of you. Owen, you are the most tender, precious little human. I love our morning snuggles, and I hope you never outgrow them. Your deep empathy astounds us. You are so intentional to remember people's names and their stories. I can't wait to see how God uses all of your many gifts. We love you so much.

To my family, thank you for allowing me to explore in the kitchen as a kiddo. You always loved and supported me and my passions. You instilled in me a belief that anything is possible. Mom and Dad, you were the best parents I could have asked for, and you're amazing grandparents.

To Chaz's family, thank you for embracing me as one of your own. You have endured our crazy eating patterns over the years and have always been so accommodating. You love our kiddos like crazy, and I am so blessed to have the best in-family in the whole world.

To my crazy amazing recipe testers, I really can't believe how much you helped me. Thank you for dedicating so much time, money and effort into this cookbook. You made this cookbook so much better, and for that I am eternally grateful. Thank you to Katrina Adlerz and Ryan Von Dohlen, Clark Boutwell, Isabel Crump, Laura Eddleman (my mom!), Laura Erickson, Michele Gornick and the Nieminen family, Jenny Hochmiller, Andrea Kelly, the Lozinski Family, Katie Mattern, Lauren McKnight, Felicia Ohnmacht, Lindsey Queener and Tim Snyder, Katelyn Pack, Taylor Pate, Dani Paulk, Erin Puckett, Kayla Rohr, Jennifer Skidmore, Abbie and Micah Sprunger, Maggie Taylor, Pam Thomas, Kristen Turner and Beth and Andrew Wadlow.

To Emily Steels, you are the best thing that has ever happened to Olive You Whole. This cookbook wouldn't be here without you. You have taught me so much with your professional skills and didn't make fun of me even once. I appreciate your dedication and friendship. Thank you!

To my friends and the communities we've been a part of in the five cities and six moves in our nine years as a family, you have loved us dearly. I am such a lucky human to have so many friends who stick by my side through thick and thin.

To my editors, Caitlin Dow and Sarah Monroe, and the entire Page Street team, thank you for believing in me, truly listening to my ideas and desires and for working so hard to make this cookbook exactly what it should be. I can't thank you enough for giving me this opportunity. To my literary agent, Jason, thank you for letting me convince you to make me your last author ever. I hope I lived up to that title and was a great final note to an amazing career.

To my photographers, Becky and Rachel, you brought this project to life. Thank you so much for the time and effort you put into making this cookbook beautiful. To my stylist and makeup artist Sineat Heintzelman, I love you so much. You really worked your magic for the cover and the lifestyle shots. You are so talented and you're an amazing friend!

Last but not least, to my readers and followers. You are why I continue to create recipes and resources. You have welcomed me and my family into your homes and your kitchen. Thank you so much for your love and support over the years.

ABOUT THE AUTHOR

Caroline Fausel is the CEO and editor of the health and wellness blog oliveyouwhole.com, where she creates healthy recipes and resources. She has always been fascinated by the search for what makes us our healthiest selves and strives to give that information to her audience. Her purpose is to help others fulfill their purposes with vitality and longevity. Caroline is Nashville-born and lives in Denver, Colorado, with her husband, Chaz, and two kiddos, Ella and Owen.

INDEX